Recalling Yesterdays

Recalling Yesterdays

Mary Joy Breton

NORTH STAR PRESS OF ST. CLOUD, INC.

St. Cloud, Minnesota

Copyright © 2014 Mary Joy Breton

ISBN 978-0-87839-754-9

All rights reserved.

First Edition: May 2014

Printed in the United States of America

Published by
North Star Press of St. Cloud, Inc.
P.O. 451
St. Cloud, Minnesota 56302

northstarpress.com

Dedicated
to my Celtic ancestors
and
to their descendants, including
my three daughters

Contents

Preface

I 'M BID 900 DOLLARS, now do I hear 950? Will ya give me fifty? Nine-fifty, nine-fifty? I hear 950, now 975, will ya give me 975, now 975?"

Of the many aphorisms of my grandmother, Lydia Ann Webster Armstrong, one that she often repeated to us was, "It's better to wear out than rust out." So far, I am grateful to say, I have been able to avoid both. But as I approach my ninth decade, I would like to record some of my life experiences.

My life has spanned one of the most event-packed and rapidly changing periods in our nation's history—multiple wars, depressions, inflations, unfathomable technological advancements (some good and some ill-advised), cultural shifts, and the coming and going of fifteen presidents. Future descendants may be interested to know about how I coped with these changes.

I am happy about the course of my experience, and I thank those who have helped to make it memorable. Sophocles said, "One must wait until the evening to see how splendid the day has been."

I hope my family and anyone else who reads my autobiography will enjoy these glimpses into the yesterdays I have experienced.

Mary Joy Breton
St. Paul, Minnesota
2014

My birthplace, 3701 Twenty-fouth Avenue South, Minneapolis, 1932.

Chapter 1

Surviving the Great Depression—
Plugging into Poverty

O N A SCORCHING AUGUST DAY in 1932, our house at 3701 Twenty-fourth Avenue South in Minneapolis came up for auction. I huddled halfway up the stairs of our two-story bungalow, waiting for a glimpse of the bird that lived in the cuckoo clock hanging on the wall above the landing. My father's nightly routine, after emptying the drip-pan under the ice box, included raising the cuckoo clock's pine-cone-shaped weights up to the cuckoo's house with the pull chains. As I watched and fantasized about the cuckoo bird—I liked to pretend it was alive—and listened to the auctioneer's chant to the crowd on the front lawn, I sensed a huge change was about to take place in my life. I didn't know what would happen to us. At eight years old, I was scared of the uncertainty. Clutching

William and Mary Dean with their family, 1928. Children, left to right: Bill, Johnny, Sandy, and me.

1

The curled crepe paper on muslin costume that my mother created for the kindergarten production of the *Wedding ofthe Painted Doll*.

my skirt to my face, I swabbed away the sweat and tears and masked my nose against the stench of cigar smoke.

The stairway was not walled, and I could peek through the balustrades, catching glimpses of the goings-on out front. In the winter we hung brown velveteen curtains in the stairwell and across the landing to confine the heat from our coal-fired furnace to the downstairs. The second-floor bedrooms were always cold. On special occasions my three brothers and I used the landing as a stage for entertaining our parents and other relatives and guests. My oldest brother, Bill, who always managed the show, had rigged a system of pull cords by which, from a spot up a few steps, he could open and close the curtains like a real stage. Another brother, Sandy, played the violin or his harmonica, while I danced free-form style in a costume made of scissor-blade-curled pink crepe paper petals sewn to a muslin base. My mother had created it for me to wear for a kindergarten performance of the *Wedding of the Painted Doll*. I played a bridesmaid and performed a between-act dance to a phonograph accompaniment of "Tiptoe through the Tulips."

Three of the family's four children were born in the upstairs front bedroom of this house that my parents bought in 1921. From this room on national holidays, my father could step through the window and edge himself along the gable of the front porch roof to slip the flag and its flagpole into a holder. He never missed a holiday.

From this open window on Election Day in 1928, my younger brother, Johnny, then two and a-half, shouted to the neighborhood in his baby voice, "Hooray for Hoover."

During the early 1930s, the iceman and the milkman still made home deliveries. The ragman in his horse-drawn wagon, the umbrella repair man, and the scissor and knife sharpener called out their hard-scrabble occupations as they made their way through the neighbor-hoods. Repair services and recycling businesses became growth industries during the Great Depression.

In the Minnesota winter mornings, we found the cardboard lids on the glass bottles of milk left on our back stoop perched atop a column of frozen cream an inch above the bottle. We sometimes mixed a bit of vanilla and sugar into the frozen cream for an "ice cream" treat. A quart of milk and an ice cream cone each cost five cents.

My father, William James Dean—five feet tall with a deep, resonant voice—had been deprived in England of an education beyond the fifth grade. He was tubercular and not expected to live to maturity. In 1898 when he was twenty-one, he immigrated to the United States. The Presby-terian Church sent him to Sisseton, South Dakota, to be a Presbyterian missionary to Dakota people. He soon abandoned that and began selling Bibles. Finally, he settled on practicing a trade—paperhanging and painting. He remained a bachelor until, at forty, he married my mother, fifteen years his junior. The four of us arrived between 1920 and 1926—just in time to be clobbered by the Great Depression. Soon after the October 29, 1929, stock market crash, my father lost his steady job at the Andrews Hotel in Minneapolis. Redecorating became an expendable luxury.

Having exhausted our savings and unable to make the mortgage and tax payments on our home, the mortgage holder was foreclosing, selling our house and most of our furnishings at a sheriff's auction.

I loved every room in that house. As I sat on those stairs, I recalled the fun we had had in the steamy warm bathroom when my father gave us our baths before story time. He would often knock on the side of the claw-footed tub as though knocking on the door of a house and then carry on an animated and comical conversation with a mysterious "Mr. Smith," who lived somewhere in the drainpipes. Mr. Smith originated as a tiny doll that had fallen off the handle of Johnny's new toothbrush and vanished down the tub drain.

After our baths, we scampered downstairs to sit on the floor around my father's easy chair while he read to us. Sometimes he read a chapter a night from *Little Women*. Or it might be a poem by Tennyson, Longfellow, or Dickinson. Two of my favorites were Longfellow's "The Children's Hour" and Dickinson's "I'm Nobody, Who are You?" My father had a way of making the stories and poems vibrant.

My parents read to us every day from the time we were infants. My mother read the poems in our favorite early childhood books so often she knew them by heart and could recite them to us as she went about her housework, while we tagged along beside her, holding the open book.

As the auctioneer's voice rang out, my mind traveled back to the way my mother had decorated our dining room for a Halloween Party she arranged for us: orange and black crepe paper streamers, hand-made pumpkin-shaped place cards and paper Halloween hats for our small guests. We played pin the tail on the donkey, blindfolded of course, and we kneeled on a chair and leaned over the back to drop clothespins in a milk bottle.

We amused ourselves in that house in other ways too. I remembered lining up the dining room chairs to play train. I stood on our large Bissell carpet sweeper for the fun of a ride as my mother pushed it over the rugs. I also recalled our summer games on the sidewalk out front: tag, hopscotch, skip-rope, and marbles.

And I saw myself sitting on my father's lap as he pushed and pulled my two main front teeth into the right position. One adult tooth had emerged in my upper front gum, and the other toward the roof of my mouth. Pushing and pulling nightly with his fingers, my father made my two upper front teeth straight and close together in only a few months' time.

Summers in Minnesota could be sweltering. Our bedrooms upstairs were always the hottest part of the house. We had no air conditioning, of course, only small floor fans. Sometimes we slept on our screened porch floor. Our bedrooms turned frigid in the winter. To warm our beds, my mother heated bricks in our gas oven, then wrapped them in newspapers and in cloth rags, pinning the rags in place with safety pins. One time, an overheated brick in Johnny's bed set fire to the newspapers and rags. Smelling smoke, my mother discovered Johnny huddled in the corner of his crib, crying while his bed smoldered. "No more bicks for me," two-year-old Johnny declared. Needless to say, henceforth she did not put hot bricks in our beds. She switched to heated soapstones.

* * * *

"SOLD! FOR ONE THOUSAND DOLLARS" the auctioneer bellowed, jolting me out of my reverie.

With our home gone and scarcely any money, my parents had to figure out what to do, where to go. While they were deciding on a plan, they rented a sparsely furnished house for the winter on Vincent Avenue in what was then a rinky-dink outlying community called Bloomington.

In Minneapolis we had traveled everywhere on foot or by trolley car. Knowing we would be without public transport in Bloomington, my folks bought an old Chevrolet. My father, already in his mid-fifties, had to learn how to drive. One day while practicing, he drove the Chevy into the alley behind our house and couldn't find—or couldn't reach—the brake pedal. The car shot straight into the lilac hedge. Certain he had killed himself, I ran screaming to the neighbors for help.

He never became a good driver. In Bloomington, if he were late arriving home after job-hunting all day, we would push the soup pot to the back of the wood-burning cookstove and stand at the window watching for our car. We could recognize its headlights turning off the main road onto the dirt one leading to our rented house. On more than one occasion, he arrived home late with a different Chevy junker than the one that he had driven away that morning. We knew then he had been involved in a mishap. One time he came home with a replacement Chevy sporting a small chrome airplane on the radiator cap. My brothers and I thought the airplane really nifty. Evidently someone else thought so too and took it, perhaps to pawn.

One frigid night, our pump pipe in the well pit froze. The next morning, my father lowered himself into the well pit to thaw out the pipe. He wrapped the pipe in rags, soaking them in kerosene and then setting fire to the rags. The rags exploded, burning my father's arms and hands as he struggled to scramble back up out of the well pit. He bore the scars of the burns the rest of his life.

The folks across the road from us in Bloomington neglected and indeed abused a little dog that hung around outside their place. Feeling sorry for the dog, we began feeding and sheltering him. He soon became our pet. We named him "Victor." With his cocked ear and markings, he resembled the image of the trademark dog inside the lid of our humpback model Victrola phonograph player.

Hoping to live off the land, my parents made a down payment on a small tract of land. Before finalizing the purchase, however, they discovered that the plot was almost solid rock and not tillable. Even so, they lost their down payment.

Early the following spring, 1933, my parents bought one acre of land for $450 from dairy farmer Willard Anderson in rural Eden Prairie Township. At that time, it was an isolated sleepy settlement on the far fringes of the Twin Cities with a population of 1,000 people. Our acre on Highway 169 sat opposite a huge Sherwin Williams Paint billboard showing paint flowing over and enveloping the Earth.

In 1853 a prominent woman author of the time—Elizabeth Frey Ellet—had suggested the name "Eden Prairie" to officials in St. Paul. She had taken a trip up the Minnesota River and described the area as the "garden spot of the territory." When the virgin prairie was in full bloom, she had climbed the river bluff. Struck by the beauty of the prairie flowers and the

Our Eden Prairie dwelling with a field of zinnias in the foreground.

panoramic view of the Minnesota River Valley, she commented to a companion that the Garden of Eden could not possibly have been more lovely. The Mdewakanton Dakota, whose homeland Minnesota has always been, call the area Wa-se-cha, "land of plenty." I remember climbing the same river bluffs as a child with my mother to look for wild flowers, especially the pale lavender crocuses with their furry petals.

7

Our one-acre plot in Eden Prairie had been planted with oats. Mother surveyed the scene, "We'll grow our food right here." It looked impossible to me. And I wondered where we would live. Even so, the prospect of a challenging new life experience somehow energized me and lifted my spirits.

A generous friend—Mr. Lathrop—who owned a lumber yard in Minneapolis, let us have enough lumber on credit to build a crude one-room shoe-box shelter and outhouse (where we recycled old Sears Roebuck catalogs for toilet paper). But we had to pay cash to the building contractor as well as to the well driller. During construction, we slept in the rental house in Bloomington. By day, we worked on clearing the weeds and oats from our acre in preparation for planting vegetables. My two older brothers—Bill and Sandy—took turns being the "horse," pulling a hand-held plough/cultivator through the sticky clay soil. Even after plowing and harrowing the ground and pulling out the oats, though, the grain kept coming back up. The task seemed overwhelming to my brothers and me, and we wanted to give up and try again the next spring. But raising vegetables meant food for the coming winter. So all of us pitched in and continued working. The sticky clay made gardening extremely difficult. Worse yet, we were inexperienced gardeners. Of the two thousand strawberry plants my mother set out, only five hundred survived the dry spring. Until we had an operating well, we hauled water in milk cans from a neighboring farm to water what we had planted.

Squatting beside my mother, I dropped seeds into the soil channel we had made with a hoe. We were creating a large bed of annuals—mostly zinnias. "Fresh-cut flowers will be our cash crop. We'll sell them along the highway."

Kind neighbors who had started a nursery business further down the highway gave us Lombardy poplar tree seedlings and small shrubs including miniature climbing roses. Roses were my father's favorite flower. His father had been a gardener on a "gentleman's estate" in Cornwall, England. On Sundays when my father dressed up for church, he liked to wear a red rose in his lapel. One of those heirloom rose bushes—after being transplanted numerous times from the garden of one descendant to that of another—thrives today under the care of my daughter, Jeannine.

We worked to enrich and aerate the clay soil on our plot by adding manure given to us by neighboring farmers. We also hauled peat from the bog in an adjacent valley. We buried our organic kitchen garbage between our vegetable crop rows and maintained a compost pile. During the summers when my mother worked in the garden, much of the housework and cooking fell to me, the only girl.

We cooked on a three-burner kerosene stove, and we used a portable metal oven over one burner when we needed to bake.

During late-summer harvest time, an oblong copper boiler covering two burners of the kerosene stove bubbled away twenty-four hours a day while my mother—often staying up all night—canned the tomatoes, corn, beans, and other vegetables we raised along with apples and peaches contributed by neighbors. We stored potatoes, squash, carrots, and cabbages in our dirt cellar under the house. One farmer gave us all the onions we could harvest ourselves. Another sold us all the asparagus we could cut for fifty cents a bushel. We bought and carried home raw milk in gallon buckets straight from the Holstein cows on a neighboring dairy farm. Cream rose to the top in a thick sheet. We skimmed it off to use on cereal and for whipping.

Butter was too expensive for us. We used oleomargarine. But in 1932, more than half the states in the country had laws prohibiting the manufacture or sale of colored oleomargarine. They imposed a consumer tax, required a license, or found some other way to restrict margarine sales. Federal agencies were barred from using margarine except for cooking. So we had to buy white oleomargarine in pouches containing capsules of food coloring that had to be kneaded into the pouch. The bans on yellow-colored margarine remained in effect until after World War II.

During our first winter in the unfinished one-room dwelling, nothing but tarpaper and thin insulation bats between the two-by-four studs sheltered us from the Minnesota cold. Sometimes snow blew in through the wall cracks onto our beds. Several of us slept on Army cots lined up along the walls. But there weren't enough cots for everyone. A large blanket chest served as an additional bed, and my younger brother, John, slept in a contraption we christened "The Chariot." We created it with an old up-holstered chair and a footstool bridged by a board. We curled up in our beds under olive-colored woolen Army blankets given to us by a relative, Colonel Sanford Parker, who had been in the 1898 Spanish-American War. He was our great uncle—the husband of Belle Webster Parker, sister of Lydia Ann Webster Armstrong, my maternal grandmother.

We had one closet for the six of us, no electricity or running water, and no indoor toilet. If it was too cold to go out to the privy at night, we used a "slop jar." My father had the unpleasant chore of carrying the slop jar out to the privy each morning. We huddled around a pot-bel-lied, wood-burning stove, which was the sole source of heat. Even when the stove was red hot as we hovered around it, our backs were freezing. I used my nightgown as a tent under which to dress and undress in a bit of privacy, shivering all the while.

Our outdoor water pump froze up every night and had to be primed each morning. That meant my mother boiled some water, and my father poured it onto the pump and well pipe. The hard well water came out a cloudy orange from the iron, which then settled to the bottom of the water pail after standing. Combined with soap (no detergents then), it produced a curd that left a ring of scum on the dishpan or all through our hair. To obtain soft water for washing our hair, we melted snow in the winter and used rain-barrel water in the summer. We washed our laundry by hand in a washtub with a scrub board, using a hand-crank wringer. In the winter, the laundry froze dry on the clotheslines.

Compared to the cute bungalow of my early years, I felt this dwelling was almost unbearably ugly. I hated it. But it sheltered us, and we were exceedingly grateful for that. We heard about many people much less fortunate than we were ending up totally homeless and having to sleep on park benches or in jail cells at police stations. According to histori-ans, the years 1933 and 1934 were the worst years of the Great Depres-sion. Although I was not yet ten years old, I realized from my parents that millions of people were suffering from poverty, hunger, and homelessness. It was a scary time.

That first summer, we did not succeed in raising enough vegetables to carry us through the winter. By November, our food supply was almost gone, and potatoes became the mainstay of our diet. Often I was still hungry after a meal, but none of us dared ask for seconds. My mother sometimes declined to take her share of the food. I think we might have come close to starving that first year had it not been for Aunt Rachel. Once a week my mother's plump sister who worked at the First National Bank in Minneapolis gave us a box of groceries. And she frequently invited us to her apartment at 2519 Hennepin Avenue in Minneapolis for a chicken or roast beef dinner on Sundays after church. She was the only member of our extended family with a steady job, and she had no husband or children to feed. My mother had been a teller at the First National Bank and had been instrumental in getting Aunt Rachel hired. My mother quit her job in 1920 at the birth of my oldest brother, William Webster Dean. Aunt Rachel remained at her job with the bank until she retired.

To my ten-year-old mind, I thought Aunt Rachel a tad bossy. She would say, "Oh, you don't want to do that," or "You don't want those," if I showed a preference for one of several styles when she offered to buy me shoes or clothes. But when I visited her in Minneapolis, she occasionally took me to see Shirley Temple movies at the Uptown Theater on Hennepin Avenue, and that more than redeemed her for me.

"When does the movie begin?"

Aunt Rachel took her feet off the Singer Sewing machine treadle for a moment. "It doesn't matter. We'll just go when we're ready."

So patching together the action of the last part of the stories with the beginning often left me confused. While I waited to leave for the movie, I entertained myself with Aunt Rachel's stereoscope. The stereoscope made two identical images appear to be one three-dimensional photograph when you looked through the lenses of the device.

Bill and Sandy hunted rabbits and pheasants in the nearby woods. My mother stretched food with bread, cracker and rice fillers: scalloped tomatoes, scalloped canned salmon, scalloped potatoes, scalloped anything. My mother baked our bread. Remembering the aroma of fresh-baked bread on arriving home from school inspired me to make bread every week during the growing-up years of my own three children.

During this stressful period, especially with so many of us living in cramped quarters, tempers could easily fly. We were not used to sharing such a small living space. I can recall one of my older brothers throwing a wash basin across the room. This made my mother take to her bed.

One evening in mid-November of 1933, as a blizzard howled outside, a loud knock at our door interrupted our story hour, making all of us jump. Laying aside the book he had been reading, my father answered the door. A stranger introduced himself as Mr. Schultz. "I'm sorry to trouble you, but I need help. My car skidded off the icy highway and rolled over into the ditch. My wife's injured and still in the car and I can't pull her out. And her shoes somehow disappeared during the accident."

Grabbing his bedroom slippers, my father followed Mr. Schultz out into the storm. They returned shortly with Mrs. Schultz propped up between them. She was in a great deal of pain.

The nearest telephone was more than a mile away at the WYE—the junction of three highways including 169 and 212. It would have been foolhardy to try to walk to it in the storm. My mother made Mrs. Schultz as comfortable as possible, but she paced the floor holding her neck most of the night. Mr. Schultz and my parents quietly talked the night hours away.

We didn't have any food to offer them.

The storm abated by morning. Mr. Shultz trudged through the snow to the Mobile service station with the flying red horse to call for help. His wife ended up being hospitalized for a couple weeks.

Just before Thanksgiving and again before Christmas, Mr. Schultz appeared at our door with huge boxes of food—fresh meat and canned vegetables, fresh fruit, and even boxes of candy. It turned out he and his wife had a grocery store in Mankato, Minnesota, and at the time of the auto mishap had been on their way to Minneapolis to purchase stock for their store. That year my three siblings and I had gorgeous fresh oranges in our Christmas stockings, plus peanuts in the shell, and chocolate candy.

While our situation gradually improved in the years following 1933, our holiday dinners that winter tasted more delicious to me than any since. The Schultzes remained longtime friends.

A friend of my father's—a fellow Cornishman—immigrated to the United States shortly after my father did. While the friend was getting established here, my father gave him some money. During our hardest Depression winter, this English friend sent us $200 for food. Later he sent $300 to help us improve our living quarters.

My father took whatever odd jobs he could line up. Often he came home after a long dry spell without work and would lie down on the big blanket chest with his face toward the wall. I knew he was not asleep. Was he crying? I wanted to comfort him, but I didn't know how. Still, each evening he read to us by kerosene lamp. One of our favorite books—a gift from a friend—was Rachel Field's *Hitty—Her First Hundred Years*. Written in 1929, the book received the 1930 Newberry Medal. It is the charming and adventurous memoirs of a wooden doll carved in the early 1820s by a Maine peddler using mountain ash wood from Killarney, Ireland. The doll and her owner, Phoebe Preble, joined Phoebe's father on a journey aboard his whaling ship, launching her adventures from one owner to another around the world. For example, once she was picked up by a mother crow and dumped into a nest to feed the hungry baby crows. She survived a shipwreck, found herself included in a snake-charmer's act, lived with some Indigenous tribes in the South Seas, and attended a concert featuring Jenny Lind, the famous and gifted Swedish opera soprano. Hitty, the antique doll on whom Rachel Field based her story, resided in a museum in Stockbridge, Massachusetts.

Through the long winter evenings, my parents devised many ways to keep us entertained. We played board games, such as checkers or caroms, tick-tack-toe, cat's cradle with string, or card games like old maid or rummy. We also hooked a rug using narrow strips of cloth cut from worn-out woolen garments. We hooked them into an English country cottage and garden design sketched by my artist mother onto a burlap gunny-sack. We played hide the spool or thimble to see who could find the object first. We played guessing games. We cut snowflake designs from folded paper, and we knitted string on a spool. Often we perused seed catalogs and the Sears "wish book." My parents made our lives fun.

Sometimes during the winter evenings, my father repaired old clocks discarded by people who had employed him. While he fixed the clocks, he listened to classical music and opera. He had only a few phonograph records, but we played them over and over on our hand-crank Victrola. One of my father's favorites was the boating song, "The Barcarolle," from Offenbach's opera, *The Tales of Hoffman*. He especially treasured his few records of the famous Italian opera tenor, Enrico Caruso (1873 to 1921). Another composition he loved was Handel's "Largo." When a family friend gave us a used piano and paid for piano lessons for me, I worked hard to learn to play the "Largo" to please my father. I enjoyed learning to play the piano, but the recitals soured me on taking lessons. So after two years of lessons, I quit, though I continued practicing on my own.

The challenge of building crystal sets captured my brothers' fancy and helped keep them occupied during the long cold winter. Crystal radios became very popular during the early days of broadcasting. They required no batteries or household electric current to operate. AM radio stations supplied the power. Crystal sets provided the first type of radios for broadcast reception and remain the simplest form of AM (amplitude modulation) receiver yet devised. Being self powered, these receivers required headphones for listening. Even though the sound was quite faint, it was still easy to hear. I remember watching my brothers Bill and Sandy peck away at the surface of the galena crystal detector with a fine wire probe called a "cat's whisker." Eventually they would hit just the right facet of the crystal to pick up a radio station.

Once we had electricity, a friend who repaired radios gave us a used one. This made winter evenings in later years more fun. We listened to the *Lux Radio Theater*, *Fibber McGee and Molly*, the *Lone Ranger*, and Jack Armstrong to entertain us, while H.V. Kaltenborn spurred discussion from his commentaries on the news. For a time, my mother and I became fans of one of the first daytime soap operas on radio—*Mary Marlin* with its "Clair de Lune" theme song by Claude Debussy.

Come spring, neighboring farmers hired Bill and Sandy to help plant potatoes, corn, and onions, bringing in a little cash for our groceries. John bagged corn tassels at the Northrup King seed proving ground. My brothers also raised and sold chickens and eggs. We all worked hard, but we were doing okay. The fears about surviving began to ease.

*   *   *   *

Over the years, we gradually improved our Eden Prairie home, until we once again had at least the basic amenities. We added a small shop to the front corner of our shoebox house close to Highway 169. My mother sold not only fresh-cut and dried flowers but also gourds she had raised from seeds that came from all over the world, producing gourds of every shape and variety. When the gourds dried out and the seeds rattled, she scrubbed off the mold and painted them, creating art objects—vases, hanging gourd strings, table centerpieces, swans, penguins, cranes, clowns, dolls, baskets, and jugs. My mother had received a scholarship to attend the Minneapolis Art Institute, during her second year. My mother was a gifted painter, so she also sold her art work—watercolor, oil, and pastel. With her diverse artistic talents, she made our humble home attractive.

I wore second-hand clothes given to me by an affluent family friend. I liked these fine-quality clothes better than the ill-fitting dresses Aunt Rachel occasionally stitched up for me. My brothers and I each had one pair of shoes a year. We extended their wear by going barefoot in the summer. When a hole appeared in the sole, we cut a piece of cardboard to fit inside. Most everyone we knew did the same. In the winter, I wore long-john underwear to school under my ribbed cotton stockings. Garters attached to a homemade contraption called an "under-waist" held up the stockings. Wearing long underwear embarrassed me. It created a telltale ridge at my ankles. But my family couldn't afford the popular snow pants.

My father wore white-bibbed denim coveralls for work that smelled of shellac and turpentine. The "hobos" who came to our door for food wore dark-blue coveralls that smelled of sweat. Most of them were unshaven. My mother always invited them in and gave them something to eat, even if it was only a cucumber sandwich. They stopped at our place so regularly I wondered if they told each other which homes were friendly. Usually they offered to do chores in exchange for food. These strangers both frightened and fascinated me. I hid around a corner and peeked at them while they ate.

Between painting jobs my father was able to line up, he worked on the interior of our own house. I liked to watch him patiently sanding, cleaning, and preparing surfaces before applying coats of paint or varnish. Sometimes he let me help. Often he whistled while he worked. That always made me happy. My father's paper-hanging table—two wooden planks propped across two sawhorses—often served double-duty as a summer picnic table outside or a holiday dining table inside. We even used it years later to serve refreshments at my garden wedding reception.

My parents did not vote for Franklin D. Roosevelt in 1932. But it was through Roosevelt's Work Projects Administration program (WPA) that my father finally obtained employment for several months, wheeling dirt with a road-repair crew. Being a rather proud person, my father did not like having to accept a public-assistance job. Stubbornly, he never did vote for Roosevelt in subsequent elections, although my mother did.

We saved and recycled everything. I didn't know you could buy elastic bands, string, paper clips, bags, and wrapping paper in stores. I thought the only way to come by these items was to save them as they came into our household.

Farmers, of course, have "recycled" their seeds since time immemorial, planting those they harvest in the fall the following spring. My mother did this too. But one year we learned how this practice can go awry if certain crops are planted too close together. We had saved seeds from one year's cantaloupe crop to use the following year, not realizing that cross-pollination had occurred between the melon and squash patches in our small garden plot. When we harvested the replanted melons the following summer, they tasted terrible. Only years later could I eat melons again.

Early each fall, my mother shepherded my brothers and me out to pick black nightshade berries. She knew where to look for them beyond our acre—in thickets, degraded woodlands, pastures, and weedy areas.

We usually filled two strawberry baskets with the small purplish black berries—enough to make a couple pies. The tradition had passed down from my grandmother. Each bite of the bittersweet pie triggered a prickly sting in my mouth. But it was still a fruit pie, and our Depression diet welcomed it. Friends thought we were mad to be eating nightshades, most varieties of which are poisonous. But my mother and grandmother knew which variety could be eaten safely when the berries were fully ripe. Some of my favorite vegetables belong to the vast family of nightshades—potatoes, tomatoes, peppers, and eggplant.

Today I sometimes see black nightshade plants growing along alleyways, in vacant lots, along old railroad lines, or in waste areas as I walk about. Although I have no inclination to collect berries for a pie, I nod my head in gratitude to this humble plant, called a weed, for its role in helping my family survive the Great Depression.

In 1940, my oldest brother, Bill, joined the Marine Air Corps, earning his wings in August 1941 at Pensacola, Florida. During World War II, he became a much-decorated Grumman torpedo bomber pilot in the South Pacific, rising to the rank of major. Our family still owed two long-outstanding debts: $500 to the Lathrop Paint and Lumber Supply Company in Minneapolis for the lumber they let us have on credit early on and for materials my father needed for whatever house painting and wallpapering jobs he could line up; and we owed Aunt Rachel for the groceries she had given us. Once Bill was receiving good pay in the Marine Air Corps, he sent a letter to Mr. Lathrop pledging to pay off our debt at fifty dollars a month. Knowing of our family's dire circumstances, Mr. Lathrop later told us he never expected us to pay the debt.

In 1942, my father accepted a temporary job in Whitehorse, Yukon, as a camp steward (a euphemism for kitchen helper) with the U.S. Army highway construction crew building the Alaska/Canada (Alcan) Highway. The pay far exceeded anything he had ever earned, and he even did some barbering on the side. But he had to work with a rowdy group and was glad to finish the assignment and return home ten months later. One of the first things he did on returning home was to repay

Aunt Rachel for the boxes of groceries she had given us during our most difficult times. When he handed her the money, she burst into tears.

*   *   *   *

The house in Minneapolis where I was born still stands and is in good condition. But our Depression-era dwelling has been razed to clear the way for an apartment complex for seniors. No longer a simple crossroads out on the prairie, Eden Prairie is now an affluent suburb of Minneapolis with a population of 55,000 (2000 census).

These childhood experiences often seemed hard to me. I saw my parents' concern. We were often hungry and cold, and I was scared. But the experiences also imbued my brothers and me with qualities and values that have served us well since: a work ethic, a sense of teamwork, an ability to conserve resources, and an understanding that imagination, creativity, and perseverance can keep us going when the money fails. We had hard times, but we had fun times too.

My portrait at ten months and ten days of age.

18

Chapter 2

Birth and Early Years

SIX YEARS AFTER THE END of World War I, a German midwife, Margarete Johannsen, attended my mother at my birth at 4:05 a.m., the morning after Thanksgiving Day—November 28, 1924. I weighed in at a hefty nine pounds. My mother later told me she wished she had known about "Dr." Johannsen when she had given birth to my two older brothers, William Webster on April 18, 1920, and Sanford James on December 20, 1921. Margarete Johannsen *did* assist at the birth of my younger brother, John Herring, who followed me by eighteen months on May 28, 1926. All four of us were born at home. I believe the main reason my mother liked Margarete Johannsen so much was because she was a student of Christian Science.

My birthday falls on Thanksgiving Day once every seven years. The story goes that my mother was so thrilled to have a girl she named me "Mary *Joy*." I have no middle name.

My mother had formal photo portraits taken of each of her four children at exactly ten months and ten days of age. As a family history enthusiast, I guess she believed it would be appropriate to have parallel photo records of her babies.

It astonishes me today to note that my birth preceded talking movies, electric refrigerators, detergents, dishwashers, washing machines and dryers, frozen foods, television, air conditioners, electric blankets, penicillin, Nylon and pantyhose, radar, credit cards, ballpoint pens, plastic, polio shots, contact lenses, Xeroxes, the moon walk, the Pill, the discovery of the planet Pluto, automatic car transmissions and turning signals, and of course FAX machines, computers, e-mail, the Internet, cell phones, smart phones, texting, Facebook, and who knows what else.

Significant events in 1924 just prior to my birth: The Russian Revolution happened only seven years before, and St. Petersburg, Russia, had been renamed Leningrad; the Winter Olympic Games were inaugurated; Calvin Coolidge became the first president of the United States to deliver a political speech on radio from the White House; the first Macy's Thanksgiving Day Parade entertained New Yorkers; Edwin Hubble announced the existence of other galaxies; George Gershwin composed the "Rhapsody in Blue"; and one of my favorite authors, Celtic novelist Rosamund Pilcher, was born two months ahead of me.

*   *   *   *

CONTRARY TO THE DEVELOPMENT PATTERN of my two older brothers, I learned to talk by my first birthday and before I learned to walk. I remained bald until I was two and sucked my thumb until I was three. In our small back yard at 3701 Twenty-fourth Avenue South in Minneapolis, my father built a playhouse and dug a pond. While my brothers sailed their paper boats on the pond, I made mud pies. One day my four-year-old imagination spiraled, suggesting that my mud pies just had to be good enough to eat. With a mouthful of mud, I scrambled up the back-door steps, howling, "Mommie! Mommie." Cleaning all the grit out of my mouth took some doing.

Our neighborhood included a number of immigrant families. A British family—the Scotts—lived across the street from us. I played with their little girl, Shirley. I envied her beautiful dark curly hair. I also envied her doll that had curly hair and eyes that opened and closed. "I'll give you my big ball," I bargained, "if you'll give me your doll." She seemed as fascinated by my large ball as I was with her doll. But our parents vetoed that deal. On my seventh birthday, however, I received a doll just like Shirley's from Mr. Scott. Thrilled with the gift, I clutched it and while racing across the street to show it to our Scandinavian neighbor, Anna Peterson, I fell flat on my face and cracked the doll's chin.

My little brother, Johnny, with his engaging smile, had captured the heart of Anna Peterson. He often sat at our window waving to her. And down the alley a few hundred yards, we discovered another Scandinavian friend, Mrs. Utheium, who grew brilliant red hollyhocks behind her cottage. Whenever I visited her, Mrs. Utheium offered me waffles or candy. I was afraid of her husband, Pete, however. One summer day, my brothers and I decided to pitch a tent in our back yard using one of our father's drop cloths. We planned to live in the tent, so I hauled all my clothes out of the house. "What do you think you're doing?" my mother asked when she saw me carrying my Sunday-best pink bonnet out the door. I took the bonnet back upstairs. After we settled in for the night, Bill, always the tease, whispered, "Pete Utheium is going to come and get you." Scared witless, I retreated to the safety of my upstairs room, soon to be followed by my brothers.

Around the corner and on the far side of our block, a Jewish couple operated a bakery. We felt very grown up when we were allowed to walk there to buy our bread. "I can eat the paper labels stuck on the loaves," Bill bragged, and he did.

The streetcar line ran not far from our house, and we could hear the trolley cars clanging down the street with their contact points buzzing on overhead wires. On Sundays, we all rode the trolley to the Christian Science church. We sat through the hour-long service followed by an hour of Sunday school. When I was a toddler, my father kept me quiet during church by holding me on his lap and letting me listen to the ticking of his large pocket watch. One Sunday when I was older—maybe seven or so—Sandy and I became convulsed with giggles over the hairy leg of a man sitting next to us.

When my parents first moved into that bungalow on Twenty-fourth Avenue, my grandmother, Lydia Ann Armstrong, and my mother's sister, our Aunt Rachel, lived with us. I remember sitting on Aunt Rachel's lap in the rocking chair, enjoying the soft cushions of her generous bust—quite a contrast to my mother's bony chest. Once our core household grew to six people, Grandma and Rachel moved into their own apartment. Sometimes I went to visit my grandmother, and we would go feed the pigeons in nearby Loring Park.

The food I hated most as a small child was boiled spinach. As I struggled to eat it, I gagged and spat it out on the floor. My mother finally gave up trying to make me eat it. Even today I dislike cooked spinach, though I enjoy raw baby spinach in salads. As for desserts, chocolate has no rival.

My parents did not believe in spanking. Discipline meant "sitting on a chair." But one time when I was cutting out paper dolls at the dining room table, my father called me to come dry the dishes in the kitchen. I said, "Okay, I'll be there in a minute." Next thing I knew my mother was chasing me around the table. I had no idea why. So I kept on running ahead of her. Finally it came out that she somehow thought I had called my father "Old Man" in responding to his request. I would never have dreamt of addressing my father that way. To begin with, I didn't think of my father as an "old man." But my mother was extremely sensitive about his being fifteen years her senior.

The two things that terrified me as a small child were the dark and thunder. The worst punishment episode of my childhood occurred when my mother shut me in a dark closet. I don't remember the nature of my purported offense, but I remember feeling I had been falsely accused. Guilty or not, my mother refused to let me out of the closet until I confessed to the wrong-doing and said, "I'm sorry."

John Bradshaw, best-selling author and personal growth counselor, characterized some mothers as duty-bound good women who can also express degrees of perfectionism, judgmentalism, and rigidity. When I read his descriptions, they resonated with the more difficult side of my experiences with my mother. She was good and dutiful, and she could also be a perfectionist, judgmental, and rigid in her views.

One of those views was that people, especially girls and women, should never get angry. When I got angry, she would say, "You're letting the devil talk to you." Then she would say to me, "Aren't you ashamed?" She told me nice little girls did not get angry. Like so many little girls, I did not learn what to do with "unacceptable" feelings, such as anger or grumpiness or sadness. To please my mother, I learned instead to push these feelings deep down inside. Being myself was conditional: my mother had expectations of how Mary's little Joy should behave. She certainly loved me, and certainly she was trying to be a good mother by molding my character, but she was a woman of her time in childrearing methods. Not until many decades later did I begin the work of developing a different relationship with my emotions.

My parents were both practicing Christian Scientists, which meant they sought healing for illnesses by working with Christian Science practitioners rather than with medical doctors and drugs. Our practitioner when I was small was "Auntie Hollis," who used meditation and prayer to help us through our childhood illnesses—measles, mumps, chicken pox, earaches, whooping cough, and scarlet fever.

* * * *

IN 1928 WHEN I WAS FOUR YEARS OLD, some friends invited our family to join them for a week's vacation at their cottage high on a hill overlooking Yellow Lake near Webster, Wisconsin. Although the distance was not great, the old train we took was slow and made many stops at dilapidated depots along the way. Our friends met us at the station in Webster, having driven there from Minneapolis by car. For the short trip from the train station to their cottage, we all jammed into their little jalopy along with a week's worth of food we had prepared in advance.

Swimming, fishing and hiking in the woods entertained us all week. Often our mother accompanied us on walks with her paints, brushes, and easel tucked under her arm. When she wanted to sketch or paint a scene, we played or relaxed in the tall grass nearby. The remote cottage location was a good habitat for wildlife. One night we heard what we thought was a wolf howling.

The cottage had no icebox. We kept milk, butter, and other perishables in a small cellar under the cottage accessed through a trap door in the floor. One morning we discovered a drowned mouse in our milk. Much as we were not a family to waste food, drinking the milk was not an option.

*   *   *   *

HOLIDAYS MEANT FUN FOR CHILDREN. Since we had no fireplace, we hung our Christmas stockings on doorknobs. My parents told us the truth about Santa Claus early on. The Christmas of 1928 was unforgettable. My artistic mother created a stunning two-story dollhouse, obviously working on it at night when the rest of us slept. She used a cardboard carton for the frame—something I would never have guessed had she not told us. Each room was wallpapered, using sheets from my father's wallpaper sample books. She made tiny furniture and decorated the walls with pictures. She painted the house white with a green roof and created tiny window boxes full of flowers. This dollhouse offered many hours of fun in the following years.

And, of course, each summer we looked forward to watching the fireworks on the Fourth of July at Powderhorn Park.

One summer my folks arranged to take us all on an excursion down the Mississippi River aboard a paddlewheel boat. I was still recovering from a stomach upset. "Perhaps you should stay home," my mother urged. But not wanting to miss any of the fun, I insisted I was well enough to go. Not quite myself yet, I absent-mindedly tagged along behind my brother Bill as he explored the boat, until I suddenly found myself in the men's bathroom. Bill turned to me, "What are you doing in here?" Jolted out of my daze, I scurried back out.

My life in those early years seemed filled with happy experiences. In 1928, we were clueless about what lay ahead for our family over the decade to come.

Chapter 3

Elementary School Angst

B EFORE I EVER SET FOOT IN MISS WYNN's first-grade classroom in 1930 at Miles Standish School in Minneapolis, I knew I hated her. My two older brothers had already brought home tales of her draconian disciplinary methods, and my mother verified them. For example, one day after walking home for lunch, my brother, Sandy, had been stomping around the house with his foot in a three-pound Crisco can. When it came time to return to school, he discovered that his shoe was stuck in the can and he couldn't pull his foot out. Eventually my mother extricated him, but since he would be late, she accompanied him to explain why to Miss Wynn. But Miss Wynn accepted no excuses for tardiness. It was an unpardonable sin punishable by the humiliation of having to sit in the corner in front of everyone. So when it was my turn to enter first grade, I crept early into her room each morning, dreading having to learn under this tyrant.

The contrast between Miss Wynn and our kindergarten teacher, Miss Heater, couldn't have been more radical. Everyone loved Miss Heater. Young, blonde, beautiful, soft-spoken, and always smiling, she truly loved children. She captured our hearts, and she had a talent for eliciting our best behavior and learning performance. My brother Bill had fallen in love with Miss Heater when he was in kindergarten, reporting, "when she leans over you can see her 'lungs.'"

Miss Wynn, on the other hand, wore a perpetual frown and a rageful red face. Her frizzy red hair stuck straight out from her head like a porcupine's raised quills. She had a cross voice. Just looking at her scared me.

She displayed a large red sign above the front blackboard chronicling absences and tardiness violations. If anyone came in late, she lectured us about spoiling her perfect record. She would then ceremoniously turn the sign over to the "tardy" side, so the entire class could share the culprit's embarrassment and shame. Thinking back, it now seems a miracle that we learned to read at all in the hostile environment she created. But we did—by the phonic method.

After Miss Wynn, I fancied that my second-grade teacher would surely offer a more pleasant experience. But again, true to my brothers' reports, Miss Holy turned out to be a holy terror—just as mean as Miss Wynn. Somehow we were supposed to begin learning basic arithmetic under her. Math has never been a favorite subject of mine, especially under the stress of timed testing. Terrified that I would not be able to finish all the problems before Miss Holy shouted, "Stop!" one day I succumbed to the temptation to begin figuring out the answers before she said, "Go," and penciling them on the palm of my left hand. Mind you, she had placed the test sheet in front of us with the examples' side up, which, reflecting back, leads me to believe she did that with the hope she might enjoy catching someone cheating. And, of course, she did catch me. As her ominous presence loomed above my desk, I knew she knew. Prying open my left hand, she displayed the evidence and fulminated my crime to the entire class. As my sweaty hands gripped the edges of my desk, her words boiled my tears of embarrassment dry.

But my chagrin over this episode paled in comparison to my third-grade mortification. By this time (1933), we had lost our house and were renting a place in Bloomington, and my third-grade teacher's name was Miss Law. She lived up to her name by enforcing rigid rules. One of Miss Law's rules was that students could not obtain permission to leave the room to go to the bathroom by raising their hand. We had to hold it and wait until recess or the lunch break to go. Obviously, this woman had never been a child.

One day the inevitable happened: I could not hold it back. A rivulet flowed along my desk seat and then trickled to the floor. It seeped down my legs, soaking my much-hated ribbed cotton stockings. My assigned desk was in the middle of the room in plain sight of everyone. As fingers pointed to the puddle and snickers rippled through the room, I felt my body heat surging upward to my already scarlet face. My trauma was such that I cannot remember what happened next, but presumably Miss Law then excused me to leave the room.

By the time I entered fourth grade, we had moved to Eden Prairie. The Eden Prairie consolidated school, a brick building set on a hill, enrolled students from grades one through twelve. Each room accommodated two grades and one teacher. Eight years later in 1941, the enrollment of the entire school totaled 199. My senior class of twenty-three students ranked the largest graduating class in the school's history to that date.

Establishing meaningful relationships with girlfriends in school was never easy for me. But several girls stand out in my memory. A brief friendship with a girl named Margie Dorn when I was in fourth grade taught me an important lesson. Things would be going along fine between us, but then she would suddenly stop talking to me. Repeatedly I would ask, "Why are you mad at me, Margie?" only to be given the silent treatment. Eventually I discovered she didn't want me to talk with anyone but her. She was possessive and controlling. For a while our relationship made my life miserable. I would arrive home from school in tears. "Just ignore her behavior and go about your own business," my mother suggested. This so-called "friendship" soon ended.

I thought we were about as poor as a family could be until my good friend Dora Hone, another classmate, invited me to dinner at her house. One thing I remember particularly about the occasion was that they used Mason canning jars as water tumblers at the dinner table. Our water glasses at home seemed elegant by comparison. Dora's older brother, Ernie, shone as a basketball star on the Eden Prairie team.

Edna Stewart and I enjoyed a long and close friendship. We remained buddies through high school. Phyllis Cook, a cousin of Minnesota Governor Harold Stassen, also became a close friend.

As for boys, I never paid much attention to them. Then, when I was in fifth grade, I noticed that a freckle-faced boy kept flirting with me.

Puppy love blossomed, though only briefly. His behavior puzzled me. One day when the teacher had stepped out of the room, he marched up and down the aisles with oranges under his pullover sweater where a girl's breasts would be. Another time he asked, "Do you know what people have to do to have a baby?" He didn't pose the question to me personally. But he spoke loudly enough so everyone in the room could hear.

Most of us at eleven years of age didn't know about sex. I was probably more ignorant on the subject than most kids. I thought babies somehow came out of women's breasts! Any other option seemed out of the question to me.

Because of her strict views about her religion, my mother taught me not to listen to my body or admit I was hurting physically or emotionally. I got the impression from her that my body, or at least certain parts of it, was dirty. She avoided any questions I asked about sex and babies. Later, when I was about to be married, she cautioned me that sex was only for having children. The only birth control she believed in was total abstinence. Not surprisingly, my father slept with my brothers in an attic room above our Eden Prairie shack and I had to share a bed with my mother.

Eventually I learned how babies were born by watching our mother cat give birth to her kittens. I had no idea how the kittens got in her in the first place. Finally when I was thirteen years old I learned about sex. I found an article in *Good Housekeeping Magazine* on how to tell your children about sex. We didn't subscribe to the magazine, but I suspect my mother—unable to broach the subject with me face to face—planted the magazine on a side table in our living room where she was certain I would find it. One hot summer day, my mother left me to monitor the cooking of some potatoes on the stove while she gardened. Engrossed in the article about sex, I became oblivious to everything else and did not smell the potatoes burning. My mother rushed into the house, her face flushed from the heat. "Couldn't you smell the potatoes burning?" she scolded. "I could smell them way out in the garden."

I began menstruating when I was twelve. Tampons were already available at that time; but my mother disapproved of them. And she either didn't approve of sanitary napkins or felt we couldn't afford them. At any rate, she demonstrated how to fold rags and pin them to one's undergarments. Soiled rags were put to soak in a covered chamber pot, later to be rinsed and wrung out by hand, then washed. Ugh! Later, after I earned my own money, I made my own decisions on the matter. The first day of my period always gave me excruciating cramps. Relief came only after I married and had my first child.

Getting back to the fifth-grade boyfriend, this freckle-faced classmate suddenly ceased talking to me. I didn't know why. Thinking back, perhaps he had become aware of the facts of life and was turned off by them. Anyway, heart-broken and in childhood anguish, I wrote him a note telling him of my heartbreak and asking him what was wrong. In the note I said, "My hand is quivering so badly I can scarcely write." Well, he showed my note to some other kids, who inevitably began teasing me, calling me "quivering hand." That ended my first love. We didn't talk to each other again until late in high school. Surprisingly, this classmate has kept in touch with me from time to time during the intervening years—the only one to do so.

In spite of these early ordeals, I loved school. And I had some admirable teachers. Miss Neva King was a truly noble soul. She taught both fifth and sixth grade in a single room in our small rural school. In her classes, we learned how to read music and how to sing in harmony. She also taught us to identify the various orchestral instruments. She brought to class her own portable 78-rpm record player. After telling us about the lives of composers as well as relating interesting background stories about the compositions, she played classical music for us. I think of her each time I hear Beethoven's *Fifth Symphony*. Learning about Beethoven's deafness when he wrote the famous *Fifth* and his inability ever to hear it performed moved me to tears.

Miss King also drilled us in the Austin Palmer Penmanship Method of muscular movement handwriting. This required correct posture, relaxation exercises, movement practice, and proper pen-holding. I can still hear Miss King chanting, "Compact ovals two spaces high, two

My teacher, Miss Dottie Nye, and our seventh and eighth grade classes, Eden Prairie, 1937. I am at the far left in the back row.

spaces high, make them light, make them light, make them light." Palmer's other basic exercise drill of straight strokes up and down and close together followed her chant of "Push, pull, push, pull."

Miss King died in her nineties, but some time before she died I wrote to her expressing my heartfelt appreciation for her substantial role in shaping my development. She sent a lovely note back to me written in perfect Palmer penmanship.

As I approached the end of my elementary school days, my seventh- and eighth-grade teacher, Miss Dotty Nye, sparked my abiding interest in nature and the environment. She took us on field trips, and under her guidance we learned to identify common bird species, trees, wild-flowers, and wildlife as well as astronomical constellations.

Encouraged and guided by my teachers and our school librarian, Ruth Willette, reading books became my absorbing passion during this period. Among my favorites: Gene Stratton-Porter's books—*Freckles* and *Girl of the Limberlost* as well as Lucy Maud Montgomery's *Anne of Green*

Gables series. Naturalist William Henry Hudson's exotic, romantic, and tragic novel, *Green Mansions*, that takes place in South America's tropical Amazon area also brought tears. But I read it several times.

Meanwhile, aside from school experiences, several events of this period remain emblazoned on my memory. In the summer of 1934 (I was ten), our entire family drove in a dilapidated 1927 Chevy to Watertown, South Dakota. We had been invited to spend a weekend at the cottage of some friends on Lake Kampeska. While we were in that region of South Dakota, we drove down to Arlington, where my grandparents had had a farm and where my mother's father, Thomas Carouth Armstrong, is buried.

*   *   *   *

In 1934 I had a traumatizing experience that haunted me for decades. It also reinforced my mother's view that anger was a bad and dangerous emotion to let loose. Here's what happened:

A man and woman standing against the balcony's marble railing on the third level of the Hennepin County Courthouse raged at each other. Their angry shouting reverberated throughout the building's somber atmosphere, blurring their words.

One level below the quarreling couple and at a right angle to them in the quadrangle, my younger brother, John, and I—nine and ten years old—also leaned against the balcony's marble balustrade. Intimidated by the solemn surroundings, we spoke to each other in whispers. "Do you think they're married? What could they be fighting about? Well, it might be money." Everyone during the 1930s worried about jobs and money.

Our two older brothers—Bill and Sandy—had been summoned to testify as witnesses to an automobile accident that had occurred on Highway 169 near our home in Eden Prairie. A drunken driver had crashed head on into another car, killing a mother and an infant girl.

While waiting for our brothers and our parents to emerge from the courtroom, John and I gazed in awe at the elaborate architecture of the courthouse, unlike anything we had ever seen before. The open quadrangle and decorative vaulted ceiling over the rotunda, the arched, stained glass windows, the geometric colored pattern of the marble floors and the marble stairways all contrasted sharply with our one-room house in Eden Prairie's farming community.

Bill and Sandy had been hunting pheasants and rabbits in the woods adjacent to the highway when the accident took place. Hearing the ear-splitting screech of tires and the deafening crash of the two cars, they had raced to the bloody scene to help. Charges against the drunken driver led to a trial, and our brothers had been summoned to testify in the criminal justice proceedings.

During the trial, John and I whiled away the time in the common area of the courthouse as best we could. We were particularly intrigued with studying the gigantic marble statue in the rotunda below us entitled, "The Father of Waters" typifying the Mississippi River. The naked figure reclined on an Indian blanket leaning against the paddlewheel of a riverboat. He grasped a mammoth corn stalk in his hand. On the rocks beneath him an alligator squirmed on top of a huge tortoise. The "Father of Waters" had a long wavy beard that rippled over his chest.

Meanwhile, the quarreling couple's vituperative behavior continued to escalate, finally riveting all our attention on them. Suddenly, the woman screamed. We watched in horror as the man flung himself over the railing, plummeting to the rotunda floor below with a dreadful thud, creating a huge pool of blood, right next to the mammoth sculpture.

The commotion sucked the courthouse hearing rooms empty as everyone scrambled out to the balconies to see what had happened. The court excused Bill and Sandy from further service. "Let's get out of here," my father said as my parents whisked us out of the building and into our old Chevy for the trip home.

Deep in shock, we rode home in silence, each in our own way contemplating what had happened and trying to process it. None of us had ever witnessed someone commit suicide. We were confronted that day with what it meant to be alive. Many decades later, the image of that terrible scene that took place in such a beautiful building remains indelibly imprinted on my psyche. My parents never talked with us about this event.

The "Father of Waters" statue, Minneapolis City Hall.

In 2000, I relocated back to the Twin Cities after living elsewhere for fifty-four years. Hoping to heal the last remnants of trauma still stuck in my psyche from this childhood experience, one morning in July 2001, accompanied by my youngest daughter, Jeannine, I revisited for the first time the scene of the suicide. The interior of the beautiful historic brownstone with its clock tower—once the Hennepin County Courthouse—had been renovated and now functioned as the Minneapolis City Hall.

As we entered the building, the "Father of Waters" sculpture in the rotunda loomed into view. I caught my breath as nausea engulfed me. I sank down onto the nearest marble bench, "I need to stop a minute, Jeannine." A few minutes later we climbed to the second floor. While standing at the balcony railing, I experienced a mental playback of the tragedy. However, my adult perspective enabled me to expand my awareness to share the pain the disaster had caused others: the man's companion and his family and friends. I pondered what he himself might have been experiencing as he fell. I also felt empathy for those who had to clean up his remains. A feeling of compassion for all these players swept over me.

Although as a ten-year-old I could not fully comprehended what happened, I realized that the experience had planted in my consciousness during my growing-up years an awareness of life's deeper issues—life and death, of course, but also each individual's value, the human body's value, the struggles we go through, and the meaning and purpose of existence in the larger scheme of things.

After an hour of walking around, taking photos, and talking with Jeannine about the incident, I felt ready to leave. I continued to process the emotions that had resurfaced while I was in the building all afternoon and into the evening. But by the end of the day, the intense feelings subsided. The pain that I had stuffed away for so many decades began to lift.

Three days later, however, during a chiropractic treatment, I told the practitioner about the experience. My body became tense, and I shook all over. As she massaged the tightness away, the tension drained, and I felt a clearing away of the trauma that had evidently been stored in my body's cells all those years.

*   *   *   *

IN THE SUMMER OF 1938, my brother Bill, now eighteen years old, took me for my first airplane ride in a small single-engine airplane with him as the pilot. Bill also taught me how to drive a car. Driver's licenses were not then a requirement, and turning signals had not yet been invented.

Minnesota, well known for its erratic and rapid weather changes, owes at least part of its cultural heritage to its snow-preparedness ethic. According to a Wikpedia article on the "Climate of Minnesota," the state's location "allows it to experience some of the widest variety in the United States." Two storms during my growing-up years etched themselves in my memory.

On the Fourth of July in 1938, just as we were about to slice the ham and serve the potato salad while picnicking with friends in our Eden Prairie garden, one of Minnesota's violent storms suddenly struck. Perhaps it was a tornado. We had no weather channel to tell us what

Me at age sixteen with my brother, Bill, twenty. Bill tied a string to the Baby Brownie camera shutter to take this photo.

happened. We later learned that the wind had been clocked at eighty miles an hour in Shakopee. The torrential rain sent us flying into the house to close all the windows. In spite of our efforts, rain poured in, soon becoming ankle deep. We all mopped wildly. The storm ceased as quickly as it began. Venturing outside, we discovered that the auto repair garage next to us, operated by our good friend Chester Brown, had been totally demolished. My brother Bill, who often worked part time for Chester, donned a bathing suit and set about salvaging whatever he could from

The high school graduation photo of my oldest brother, Bill, 1938.

the debris. The only items he found anywhere near intact included a peanut machine, which dispensed some peanuts for a penny, the cash register, and a few tires. For weeks afterward, we found debris in our yard and far out into the onion field in the peat bog valley that stretched behind our acre. While rummaging barefoot among the debris behind the demolished garage, I stepped on a nail.

Minnesota's worst blizzards have followed a parallel pattern: unseasonably warm temperatures followed suddenly by rain, then sleet, then rapidly plummeting temperatures accompanied by snow and high winds, often creating white-out conditions. The November 11, 1940, Armistice Day Blizzard conformed to this pattern. Inadequate weather forecasting systems and warnings led to treacherous situations and indeed deadly outcomes. I remember it well. I was sixteen years old.

With mild morning temperatures, duck hunters ventured out without adequate clothing. Twenty hunters lost their lives in this blizzard. One hunter attributed his survival to his two large Labrador hunting dogs that snuggled on each side of him as he lay in the snow, preventing his freezing. The total death toll in Minnesota alone climbed to forty-nine. The storm, blazing a thousand-mile wide path through the Midwest, took the lives of 154 people. Two people died when two trains collided in the blinding snow. And poultry farmers suffered the loss of more than a million turkeys.

A woman in suburban Bloomington, Minnesota, recalled her father coming in from the storm with his overcoat encased in ice. He stepped out of his coat and the coat just stood there by itself, frozen on the spot.

My grandmother, Lydia Ann Webster Armstrong, described how, in the mid 1800s, my grandfather would secure a rope between their house and the barn on their South Dakota farm whenever a blizzard approached. During whiteout conditions, this ensured that he could make it to the barn and back safely to care for his livestock.

The now famous 1940 Armistice Day Storm ranks number two on Minnesota's climatology chart of weather events in the twentieth century, second only to the Dust Bowl of the 1930s. The storm, categorized as a "cyclonic blizzard," has been called one of the deadliest storms of the country up to then. After a freezing rain, snow fell up to twenty-seven inches in some areas, accompanied by winds fifty to eighty miles per hour creating twenty-foot drifts. The fifty-degree (Fahrenheit) rapid temperature drop within the space of only a few hours caught everyone unprepared.

Stories about the storm have remained a topic of conversation ever since. I have a photograph taken by my mother after the storm. In the photo, two of my brothers, my father and I stand on top of a huge snowdrift by our back door in Eden Prairie. Our old Chevy sits partially buried under the same snowdrift.

Shortly after the Armistice Day Storm, an editorial

My dad and two of my brothers and me standing on a snow drift after the famous Armistice Day Blizzard of 1940.

appeared in the *Minneapolis Star-Tribune*: "It takes an old-fashioned blizzard to bring out the unbeatable spirit of Minnesotans. We've praised the spirit of Londoners (during the Blitz), but Minnesotans can 'take it' too."[1]

[1]Bruce White, "Blizzard Tale from Minnesota," *Minnesota Star Tribune*, MinnesotaHistory.net, December 13, 2010. For more information on this blizzard, see *Wikipedia*, "Amistice Day Blizzard," http://eb,wikipedia.org/wiki/Armistice_Day_Blizzard (accessed October 6, 2013).

Chapter 4

Celtic Lineage

BEFORE CONTINUING STORIES ABOUT MY LIFE, I should describe my family's background—how we came to this continent and moved around on this land. First, I want to tell about my mother, Mary Mercy Armstrong Dean.

My mother's ancestor, Robert Herring, five generations preceding her, emigrated from Leeds, Yorkshire, England, to the United States in 1720. His descendant, my maternal great-grandmother, Mercy Haskell Herring, was born in 1815 in Bangor, Maine, and she relocated with her family from Maine to Durand, Illinois, around 1820. An antique chest of drawers that traveled with the family across the plains in their oxen-drawn covered wagon from Maine to Illinois has served as my bedroom dresser for many years. My mother named my younger brother, John Herring Dean, after Mercy's father, John R. Herring.

Until five years before her death in 1876, Mercy Haskell Herring penned a diary. Fortunately I have those records. These fragile volumes provide a rich source of information for me about her life and about that period in our history. Here is what they reveal about her life.

Mercy Haskell Herring attended a Friends Boarding School in Providence, Rhode Island, for a couple years when she was in her early twenties. Her autograph book includes messages dated 1837 and 1838 from fellow students and friends. I suspect she learned the beautiful script penmanship evident in her diaries while at Friends Boarding School. Some of her handwriting resembles the Spencerian style developed a bit later, around 1850. The so-called Golden Age of American penmanship spanned the years 1850 to 1940.

In 1853, Mercy married late at the age of thirty-eight. Her husband, Price Blinn Webster, a farmer eight years her senior, had been married and widowed twice previously and already had several children. The names Abel, Minor, and Sarah—presumably children of Price's earlier marriages—crop up in Mercy Herring's diary. She wrote about sewing and "mending for Abel— pants, coats, stockings . . ." and about their visiting.

Between 1853 and 1861, Mercy and Price had four children, three girls and a boy, all born at home. The baby boy, named Granville after one of Mercy's brothers, lived only six months. The girls were: Belle, born in 1854; Julia, 1856; and Lydia Ann, my grandmother, born on August 1,

The antique chest that traveled with my great-great-grandparents from Maine to Illinois by an ox-drawn covered wagon, 1820.

1861, when her mother, Mercy, was forty-six years old. Lydia Ann, an undersized newborn, weighed only two pounds at birth. Mercy placed her in the warming oven above the wood-burning cook-stove, a common practice at the time. I recall my grandmother chanting, "I was born in 1861, the year the Civil War begun."

Mercy Haskell Herring Webster's life spanned the Civil War period. She often referred to the war in her diary entries:

> Friday, January 1, 1864: "At the commencement of last year many thought before the commencement of another year peace would be restored, but alas the same dark heavy cloud hangs over us and I fear another year will commence its flight before Peace and order will be restored. O unhappy country, when will men learn to live as they ought?"

February 3, 1864: "I wrote a letter to brother Benjamin today. How I wish I could see the poor boy. When will this cruel war come to an end."

Tuesday, May 10, 1864: "We hear that they are fighting and have been this day or two. When will this cruel war come to an end and the sound of peace once more be heard in the land? May God speed the day. I fear that years will not end the conflict."

May 13, 1864: "We hear of the capture of Jefferson Davis, the Southern President."

Monday, July 4, 1864: "The 4th of July has again returned and still this awful war with all its horrors hangs over our heads and no prospects of soon closing. We hear every day of many being slain on the field, some of our own brothers, neighbors and friends. When will it end?"

April 14, 1865: "Today we have heard of the death of our president, how horrible. He fell a victim to Southern revenge and has left a nation to mourn his loss."

Thursday, June 1, 1865: "Very pleasant, the birds sing this morning sweetly, and we all feel to rejoice that the war is over."

On a lighter note her diary entry for August 1, 1865 reads: "Today is Lydia Ann's birthday. She is four years old today and as bright and smart as you will often find of her age. She has been very sick with the Chicken Pox but is better. She stood in a chair this morning and washed the dishes for Belle to wipe; she can wash, cook, mop, sweep, iron, make beds, feed chickens, and bring wood and chips for me every day and many other chores."

Her entry for Christmas described what the children found in their stockings: "Monday, December 25, 1865. Christmas morning. Pleasant and mild. The children are pleased with the contents of their stockings. Lydia's contained a whistle shell, little iron kettle, a small earthen vase, candy, popcorn, nuts, a hickory nut doll."

She recorded in her diary the hardships of life on their large farm outside Durand, Illinois. In addition to the usual home management and child-rearing chores, such as cooking and baking, washing clothes (by hand), ironing (using a flatiron that had to be heated on the wood stove), cleaning and mopping, she also made soap, and churned butter. In the back of her diary, she recorded a chronology of the butter she churned, who bought it, and how much they paid. The family also raised cattle, sheep, horses, hogs, chickens, and geese on the farm. She carded wool from the sheep, spun stocking yarn, dyed fabric: "I am coloring black today for my carpet," she wrote. She wove on her loom, and described "sewing carpet rags what time I can get." She also double-twisted and spooled yarn to knit into garments. She made quilts, sewed clothes, "tried lard," preserved fruit from their orchard, and grew flowers in her garden. They raised the usual array of farm crops, including oats, wheat, hops (for beer), corn, and clover. She sometimes had to cook for a crew of threshers.

Occasionally an entry in her diary relates spending the day at home reading nonfiction books. She specifically mentioned *The Magic Staff*, Andrew Jackson Davis's autobiography (1826 to 1910). Davis was an American spiritualist much influenced by Emanuel Swedenborg and by the Shakers.

Lydia Ann, the youngest and last child, cared for a pet heifer named "Mary," who gave birth to a calf when Lydia Ann was seven years old—an exciting and memorable event. All the while, Mercy Haskell Herring Webster had to deal with the illnesses of her children—measles, chicken pox, small pox, mumps, scarlet fever. She sometimes sat up all night with a sick child, as she did with Lydia Ann who had scarlet fever when she was six. Mercy herself had poor health. Many entries in her diary mention her feeling "unwell": "I am quite miserable, obliged to keep Belle from the hop field to help me," (September 7, 1867). Both of her older

Lydia Ann Webster, 1867, my maternal grandmother when she was six years old.

daughters, Belle and Julia, assisted her with the housework as well as with farm chores. In addition, her husband, Price, often arranged for someone to come in to help his wife, especially with sewing. He bought a Singer Sewing Machine. "I have been sewing on the sewing machine today" (March 7, 1867). "Mrs. Peck is here today instructing Mrs. Kennedy how to cut dresses by a moddle [sic]," (April 2, 1868).

Entry for Saturday, May 11, 1867: "My mother would have been eighty-three years old today if she had been living. She is in that country where time has never entered, where years dwindle to moments and a moment grows to the length of ages, where the past and future meet in one eternal present." Mercy describes her mother's death on July 20, 1866, at age eighty-two in some detail in her diary.

July 13, 1867: "Mrs. Pottle from Maine came to make us a visit—also a colored lady, a physician, was with them by the name of Nauson." July 14, 1867: "Price and I took a ride over to Sibyl's [her sister] this afternoon and the colored lady went with us. Then we met Aunt Julia [another sister], Leonard and Rose, and she went home with them." During the first half of 1868, an orphan boy of color named Addison lived with the family.

July 27, 1867: "I warped my carpet today" [on her loom]. July 29, 1867: "Put my piece in the loom today." October 4, 1867: "Today is my birthday. Over half a century has elapsed since I was numbered with the inhabitants of this earth. How many improvements (yes to us they are new) both in the arts and sciences, political and religious institutions." March 22, 1868. (Price's sixty-first birthday). "Lydia made him a nice pen wiper." She mentions an almost total eclipse of the sun on Saturday, July 7, 1869. "The hens went to their roosts, some stars were seen." I discovered a thick lock of chestnut-colored hair (unidentified) about four inches long placed in the diary next to the entry for Thursday, November 19, 1868. I speculate that it was probably Mercy Haskell Herring Webster's own hair.

Celebrating wooden wedding anniversaries, crystal anniversaries, silver and golden wedding anniversaries offered popular occasions for community parties. In the winter, sleighing with bells on the horses became an exciting recreation.

Spiritualism and clairvoyance captured Mercy and Price Webster's interest. They sometimes went to lectures on these subjects. One clairvoyant visitor wrote a message while she was their houseguest. It was on a loose-leaf sheet of paper inserted in the diary. They also attended temperance lectures at the schoolhouse.

Mercy Haskell Herring Webster's last diary entry was dated September 23, 1871. She passed on five years later in 1876 when my grandmother, Lydia Ann, was fifteen years old. My grandmother began teaching school when she was sixteen. With the first money she earned, she bought a small Victorian side table. That table graces my own living room today.

Like her mother, Lydia Ann remained single longer than most young women of that era. In 1889, at the age of twenty-eight, she married my grandfather, Thomas Carouth Armstrong, age twenty-six, who at the time lived in Hampton, Iowa. Apparently Lydia Ann had followed her older sister, Belle, to Hampton, Iowa, where Belle lived with her husband, Lt. Col. Sanford J. Parker (for whom my brother, Sandy is named). Lydia Ann met and married Thomas Armstrong in Hampton.

In my bedroom atop the antique chest of drawers that came across the plains in the covered wagon, I have a set of two blue hand-painted porcelain perfume bottles and a matching powder jar that my grandfather gave to my grandmother as a wedding gift.

Thomas Carouth Armstrong's father, James L. Armstrong, had been born in County Donegal, the northernmost promontory of Ireland, in 1828, and he immigrated to the United States around 1860. He and his wife, Mary Carouth, also born in Ireland, first went to

Uncle Fremont Armstrong on his family's South Dakota farm in 1916 when he was twenty-one

Ohio where, in 1863 the first of their five children, Thomas Carouth Armstrong, my grandfather, was born. I recall my grandmother, Lydia Ann, quoting her husband Thomas Carouth, "The Armstrongs came from Donegal where we ate potatoes skin and all." After living briefly in Hampton, Iowa, the family settled on a homestead in Arlington, South Dakota.

Thomas Carouth and Lydia Ann had four children, the first two of whom were born while they still lived in Hampton, Iowa: Alton Alvin, born in 1890, and Mary Mercy (my mother) born on August 5, 1892. The third and fourth children arrived after the family relocated to Arlington, South Dakota: Fremont Sanford born in 1895, and Rachel born in March, 1897.

They bought a large farm near Arlington and managed to eke out a living in spite of droughts and grasshopper infestations. When crops failed, my resourceful grandfather pursued alternative means to earn money. For example, he produced cheeses.

But in May 1897, when their youngest child was six weeks old, tragedy struck. My grandfather had hitched two colts to a buggy and was out riding with them as part of getting them used to being harnessed. His two older children—Alton and Mary—were in the buggy with him. The traces—the straps connecting the colts' harnesses to the buggy—snapped. The frightened colts bolted and took off at a gallop. "Jump out—quick—jump out," my grandfather shouted to the children. Then, struggling to stop the colts and prevent their running away, my grandfather gripped and jerked on the reins with all his strength. But the colts pulled him off the buggy seat and then dragged him for a considerable distance over a rough road, causing internal injuries.

My grandfather, a strong and healthy young man of thirty-three, a teetotaler and non-smoker, had never been sick. A quack doctor made a brew of tobacco and whiskey and not only poured it down his throat but pumped it into his rectum. After he had been declared dead, he sat up in bed and said "I'm *not* dead." My grandmother firmly believed that his body would have mended itself had he been spared the quack doctor's ghastly toxic nostrum and simply received her own simple nursing care.

His untimely and heartbreaking death devastated my mother, who was then just over four years old. He had always been especially demonstrative in showing his affection for her—something my grandmother, Lydia Ann, for some reason found difficult. It was just not her nature.

My father, William James Dean, was born on June 29th, 1877, in the tiny village of Tregellan, near Scorrier, in the County or Duchy of Cornwall, England. The family's village lay in the heart of the tin and copper mining district. My father was the second of seven children—five boys and two girls—born to John Thomas Dean and Mary Ellen Manley Dean. Genealogical records suggest that the family name might originally have been "Endean."

Cornwall lies at the extreme southwest corner of England. It is a peninsula jutting out into the Atlantic Ocean, fringed by a spectacular coastline. Most of the coastline consists of cliffs. It is a part of England where myth and reality have coexisted for centuries as tangled as the roots of the gnarled old oak trees bulging up through the country's narrow roadways. The coves of the southern coast once sheltered smugglers and pirates.

Warmed by the Gulf Stream, Cornwall's mild and rainy climate produces lush vegetation, including an abundance of flowers—heather, gorse, rhododendrons, camellias, roses, magnolias, azaleas, anemones, geraniums, primroses, and many others. In the typical English cottage garden, flowers flourished right amongst the vegetables. Some varieties of flowers help control pests. I remember hearing my father say that *his* father had been a gardener on a "gentleman's estate."

* * * *

IN SEPTEMBER 2004, I attended a Ramsey County Garden Club meeting in St. Paul, Minnesota, featuring a speaker from England who gave a talk about English cottage gardens. In his historical review, he talked about the lives of the working class in past centuries and how they used the products of their gardens.

He said that because baths were infrequent (once a week at best), cottages could become rather smelly. Gathering lavender from the garden, folks spread the cuttings on the floor and then tromped on them. The rising lavender fragrance, if not overriding the unpleasant odor, at least helped mask it.

He talked about porridge, a staple food among the working class. Ground cereal, often oats, could cook for more than a week on the stove. Throwing some leeks, peas, and other vegetables from the garden, and perhaps a chicken into a pot of water, the porridge simmered over the fire constantly. A day or two into the cooking, some barley might be added to the soup making it thicker and more like a stew. In this way, the porridge could be extended as the days passed. Peas constituted a standard ingredient. Hence the nursery rhyme "Peas porridge hot, peas porridge cold, peas porridge in the pot nine days old."

* * * *

THE CORNISH LANGUAGE, one of the Brythonic dialects of Gaelic, is related to the Breton and Welsh languages. Cornish folks have a characteristic manner of speaking. They drop their "h's" for one thing. My father endeavored to eliminate any traces of a Cornish dialect from his speech. And he pretty much succeeded.

Some years ago, the PBS Masterpiece Theater series, *Poldark,* was set in Cornwall's mining district, and our family was hooked on watching it. Recently, the PBS series *Doc Martin* was also set in Cornwall, and we loved watching it as well.

But life during my father's childhood was tough for Cornwall families. From an early age, most of the boys and men worked in the mines. Miners had to climb down ladders instead of riding in elevator cages to reach the shallow tin and copper mines. Already flagging in energy from a long, hard day's labor, climbing back up out of the mine pushed their endurance.

Cornish pasties, a favorite and standard food found in the lunch buckets of many miners, could be savory or sweet. One of the first things my father did after marrying my mother was to teach her how to make Cornish pasties. He even requested them for his last meal before he died.

* * * *

WHILE STILL IN HIS TEENS, my father clerked and also delivered groceries with a donkey cart in St. Day, Cornwall. The Presbyterian Church attracted him, and he preached many times in a large church in St. Day. When my father was in his sixties, my parents traveled back to Cornwall and visited this church in St. Day. My father said the village looked the same as it had when he preached there as a young man.

Because my father was a sickly child and suffered from tuberculosis, he attended school only through fifth grade. Then his father pulled him out and apprenticed him to a paint shop for four years—without pay. His parents doubted he would live to maturity, so they considered further education unnecessary.

An assignment to preach in a Presbyterian Church in Sisseton, South Dakota, triggered my father's decision to emigrate. Leaving his family in Cornwall must have been heart-wrenching, especially saying goodbye to his little eight-year-old sister, Carrie, whom he adored. Nevertheless, in 1898, at twenty-one years of age, he boarded the steamer St. Paul sailing for the United States. On arriving, he traveled directly to Sisseton, South Dakota. He applied for citizenship a few years later and became naturalized in Watertown, South Dakota, on March 13, 1912.

In the meantime, on August 27th, 1907, my father filed for 160 acres of land under a series of Homestead Acts (the first passed by Congress in 1862). He filed four years after the infamous 1903 Lonewolf v. Hitchcock case, in which the U.S. Supreme Court ruled that Congress had "plenary power" over Native nations. That meant Congress could pass any law affecting Native Peoples without their consent, even laws that entailed the wholesale theft of their treaty-guaranteed lands through "homesteading." Under the 1868 Fort Laramie Treaty, more than half of what is now called South Dakota remains the rightful territory of the Oceti Sakowin Oyate, the Dakota, Lakota, and Nakota nations. Yet Congress stole it and gave it to white settlers, my father being one of them.

Gaining title to the so-called "unoccupied" acreage of "public land" required five years of residency. As far as I can determine, my father never fulfilled the residency requirement, and I'm glad he didn't. I feel shame about our history of crimes and injustices against Native Peoples, but I also know that honest and well-founded shame means little unless it moves me to act to mend harms and to put things right. This awareness motivates much of my work today.

After my father came to the United States, he regained his health. He attributed this to his study of Christian Science. He gave up preaching and sold Bibles for a time. Ultimately, after settling in Watertown, South Dakota, he returned to working the trades he had learned in England—paperhanging and painting.

These roots in England and Ireland defined my lineage from Celtic roots. I do not know the language of Cornwall. The last speakers are very old, and many have passed on. Nor do I know Celtic ways. But the lands and histories of the Celts live in me, even in my body and blood. I know this because of its downside, which I experienced during my seventh decade. More on that later.

* * * *

My grandmother, Lydia Ann Webster Armstrong, working on their Arlington, South Dakota, farm.

FOR A TIME, MY WIDOWED GRANDMOTHER, Lydia Ann Webster, now with four young children, the eldest scarcely seven years old, remained on the farm, managing it with the help of hired farm hands. Following the custom of the time, my grandfather's brother, Robert John, three years younger than Thomas Carouth, offered to marry Lydia Ann after Thomas's death. But Rob was already engaged to Daisy Phelps, and my grandmother did not want to prevent their marriage, so she declined.

My grandmother soon realized she needed additional sources of income to support herself and her children. So she leased out some acres of the large farm she had inherited from her husband. She supplemented that income by doing midwifery. She'd had a difficult labor with her own first child. The midwife attending her failed to properly stitch up a vaginal rip. While this made all her subsequent childbirth experiences easier, it allowed the organs in that part of her body to drop too low, causing problems for her the rest of her life.

Shortly after becoming a widow, my grandmother developed a tumor in her stomach. Seeking healing, she traveled to California to confer with a doctor recommended by her relatives there. While in California, she learned about Christian Science, which had become a growing movement during that period. Figuring she had nothing to lose, she decided to give it a try. The tumor dissolved, and she returned home healed.

Several years after returning to South Dakota, she sold the farm and moved her family to a rental house in Brookings, South Dakota. My mother used to tell horrifying stories about how they struggled to purge bedbugs from the house. After several years in Brookings, the family relocated to Watertown, South Dakota. My father first met my mother in Watertown while he was doing some paperhanging work at their home. Although my mother was a young teenager at the time, my father, fifteen years her senior, decided he wanted to marry her when she grew up. So he waited.

In the meantime, both my mother's family as well as my father moved to Minneapolis. In her late teens, my mother learned about scholarships to attend the Minneapolis Art Institute. She applied for one and received a scholarship for her second year at the Institute. She advanced to the life studies portion of her training. She had no clue beforehand that naked live models posed in the life studies classroom. As an extraordinarily modest young woman herself and never before having been exposed to nudity, she was totally shocked and unprepared when she walked into the classroom. Standing aghast at the sight, she dropped her drawing board and all her drawing pencils, which crashed to the floor. I believe she did well in that class, but it was many years before she showed me her sketches of nude models. She explained to me how embarrassed she had been and apologized for having had to do such drawings. She eventually destroyed them. Not surprisingly, her watercolor, oil, and pastel artwork focused exclusively on still-life arrangements, flowers, and landscapes.

Wanda Gag became a close friend of my mother's at the Art Institute. Wanda Gag, authored children's books and was a talented artist. Her most well-known book, *Millions of Cats*, first published in 1928 by Coward-McCann, received a Newberry Award in 1929 and is the oldest American picture book still in print.

In 1917, while World War I raged in Europe, my father and mother became engaged. My mother, then a student at the Art Institute, was twenty-five years old, my father forty.[2]

My father felt it was his patriotic duty to enlist in the Army, but he was under height at only five feet, underweight, and over age for military service.

The wedding portrait of my parents.

At first, the Army refused to accept him; but after he added some weight by gorging, they finally agreed to let him enlist in Battery C, Eighty-third Field Artillery stationed at Fort Sill, four miles from Lawton, Oklahoma. Anticipating the possibility of being sent overseas and perhaps being killed in combat, my father wanted my mother to be his beneficiary. So my mother traveled to Lawton, Oklahoma, where they married on September 7, 1918.

He *did* go overseas, but World War I ended on November 11, 1918, two months after they married. After being discharged from the Army at Camp Knox, Kentucky, on February 17, 1919, my father returned to Minneapolis and to my parents' first home, an apartment at 132 West Thirty-second Street. Their first child, William Webster Dean, my oldest brother, arrived on April 18, 1920. In 1921, my parents bought the bungalow in Minneapolis at 3701 Twenty-fourth Avenue South.

[2]*Wikipedia*, March 13, 2013.

Chapter 5

World War II and High School

T HE SAME YEAR I ENTERED HIGH SCHOOL—1939—Europe found itself sliding toward a nadir that none of us ever imagined possible. Germany's dictator, Austrian-born Adolph Hitler, had
already established concentration camps, where he was interning,
among others, political opponents, Jews, Communists, Romani people,
homosexuals, mentally or physically disabled people, Social Democrats,
Polish intelligentsia, and labor unionists.

Stories about the atrocities that Hitler's Nazis were committing came
trickling out of Europe, but we thought they must surely be rumors or
merely anti-German propaganda. The propaganda machines on both
sides had pushed stories of atrocities to absurdity during World War I.
So we were wary and unsure about what to believe.

One story I'll never forget reported that the Nazis had created lamp
shades from human skin. Only later did we receive confirmation of the
"Final Solution" extermination programs of the Nazis. Although most
Americans were not aware of it, the Nazi death camps were inspired in
part by a 1916 book on white supremacy written by an American racist,
Madison Grant. Hitler wrote to the author stating that his "wonderful
book," *The Passing of the Great Race*, was his "Bible."[3] Nor was Grant an
outlier or lone racial extremist in his views. The United Staes had carried out a policy of genocide and ethnic cleansing against Native Peoples
and nations. Alexander Ramsey, the governor of Minnesota, declared
to the Minnesota state legislature in 1862: "The Sioux Indians of Min-

[3]Wikipedia, Madison Grant Legacy, March, 13, 1913.

nesota must be exterminated or driven forever beyond the borders of the state."[4] Even though I grew up in Minnesota, I was ignorant of this. None of my teachers ever talked about our treatment of Native Peoples, nor did these events and policies appear in my history books.

In fact, the United States was guilty of racial persecution during World War II as well. President Roosevelt ordered that Japanese-Americans—U.S. citizens—on the West Coast be rounded up under military guard and relocated to inland prison camps, confiscating their property and businesses.

The early years of World War II terrified me. The United States had been ill-prepared. Hitler's "blitzkrieg" was gobbling up Europe. Great Britain was on the verge of collapse, and, after the United States entered the war following the 1941 Japanese bombing of Pearl Harbor, the United States was losing one battle after another in the Pacific. The chances for a favorable outcome seemed slim. What if we lost this war? I shrank from even imagining what the consequences might be.

* * * *

YET BACK IN EDEN PRAIRIE, school continued as usual. During my freshman year in high school, I began learning touch-typing and Gregg shorthand from Miss Olson in preparation for a secretarial career. I remember well the typing exercises we practiced on our Woodstock manual typewriters to burn into our body memory the location of each new letter we learned on the keyboard. Over and over, we typed: "if-it-is-in; if-it-is-in." By the end of my sophomore year, I had achieved a typing speed of sixty-five words per minute, and a shorthand speed of 120 words per minute. Today, with the advent of computers, shorthand skills have faded as a requisite qualification for specialized office workers. Nevertheless, throughout my career—and even today—the skill has remained useful, especially during telephone conversations.

During my sophomore year, Ruth Leadbeater taught a class in English composition that triggered my interest in creative writing. Miss Lead-

[4]Special session of the Minnesota legislature, September 9, 1862.

beater's curriculum for the year required that we write eight essays, a play, and an autobiography. My collection of the year's writings, which I bound in a booklet, won third prize at the Hennepin County Agricultural Society's annual fair.

Miss Leadbeater crushed me, though, when she falsely accused me of plagiarizing one of my essays—"A Day in New York City." I had never been to the city and she knew that. However, I explained to her that I had based my essay on a detailed account told to me by my Aunt Rachel, who had visited New York City during her vacation that year. Aunt Rachel was one to remember many details. Though she did not apologize, Miss Leadbeater accepted my explanation.

On reading over this collection today and after having become a published author of a number of newspaper and magazine articles as well as a nonfiction book, *Women Pioneers for the Environment* (Northeastern University Press, 1998), the essays naturally sound amateurish. But at age sixteen, those high school assignments launched my serious pursuit of writing. And for that I remain forever grateful to Ruth Leadbeater.

In Miss Peterson's literature class, our studies included Chaucer and Shakespeare, as well as a number of poets—Elizabeth Barrett Browning and Robert Browning, Henry Wadsworth Longfellow, William Butler Yeats, James Russell Lowell, Oliver Wendell Holmes, Alfred Tennyson, Walt Whitman, William Wordsworth, and William Cullen Bryant. As I name these authors today, I am aware of how "white" and Eurocentric this list is, wonderful as these authors are, and how far our curriculum has come in exposing today's students to a diversity of cultures and their literature.

Miss Peterson required that we memorize some poems or parts of poems. We didn't have to memorize any of "The Highway Man" by British poet Alfred Noyes, but the dramatic tragedy of the poem fascinated us. It's about a highway robber in love with an innkeeper's daughter who kills herself to warn him of an ambush by British soldiers. He ends up being shot anyway trying to escape. I recalled that in Lucy Maud Montgomery's novel *Anne of Green Gables*, which takes place on Prince Edward Island in the Maritime Provinces, Anne recited "The Highway Man" with distinction at the White Sands [hotel] Benefit Concert.

One of Elizabeth Barrett Browning's "Sonnets from the Portuguese,"—Sonnet Number XIV—resonated with my sixteen-year-old romantic sense. It's the one that begins,

> If you must love me, let it be for nought
> Except for love's sake only.

My enchantment with that sonnet probably stemmed from my crush on my math and geometry teacher, Conley Engstrom. He was young and single. My concentration was so distracted that my grade in geometry plummeted.

During two years of French classes, I established a pen pal in Switzerland. He wrote to me in French, and I wrote to him in English, and each of us benefited from having to translate our letters back and forth.

The girls in my class endured humiliation and disgust when several of the boys were caught spying on the girls in the bathroom. The janitor's closet adjacent to the girls' lavatory had a small hole around the commodes' plumbing pipes through which the boys peeked. None of us knew who among us had been spied on.

One day during my junior year, an emergency telephone call from my mother to the school office pulled me from class. My father, then sixty-five years old, had fallen from a scaffold, fracturing his skull and injuring his brain. The doctors suggested to my mother that he might not survive. He remained unconscious in the hospital for several days. A nurse had to install a catheter. In his delirium during the process, he admonished the nurse, telling her "that's not nice."

My mother stayed in the hospital with him twenty-four hours a day, helping to nurse him. The doctors told her that if he survived, he would never be able to work again. But in two months, he was back on a job. He worked as a laborer until he was seventy-five years old. His last employer was the Minneapolis Moline farm machinery manufacturing plant in Hopkins, Minnesota. After retiring, he continued living an active life until he died at ninety.

During all four of my high school years, I participated in the Glee Club, my favorite extracurricular activity. On one occasion, the Glee Club traveled by bus to another school to present a joint concert with their Glee

Club. One of my classmates suggested that a few of us skip out and go to a movie playing at a theater adjacent to the school we were visiting. Uncomfortable with the notion, but failing to listen to my intuition, I allowed pressure from friends to persuade me to go along with them. While we were watching the movie, we saw our Eden Prairie school superintendent, Mr. Sam Mitchell, walking up and down the aisles looking for us. Later I learned that he had made the comment to someone that he "never would have expected Mary Joy Dean to do such a thing." I was so ashamed.

All my brothers played on the Eden Prairie basketball and baseball teams. My brother Sandy in particular exhibited leadership in athletics. After doing some research, he suggested the name "Eden Prairie Eagles" for the basketball team. He also took a leadership role in laying out a baseball diamond—clearing away the rocks, raking the ground, and measuring the stretches between the bases. Since the baseball team initially had no sponsors, the team members bought their own baseball gloves and bats.

Although I lacked much athletic ability, I did play on the girls' softball and basketball teams. My interest leaned more toward dancing, for example learning the steps for the waltz, polka, foxtrot, and schottische. When the school gym was available during the noon hour for dancing, our gym teacher often coached us. I also enjoyed acting and played roles in two class plays. The members of the cast for our senior class play, *Gabriel Blow Your Horn*, gave our drama director, Miss Workman, a pair of Nylon hose as an appreciation gift. Nylons were a highly prized item, because they were next to impossible to purchase during World War II.

My brother, Sandy, Eden Prairie baseball team.

My World War II ration book.

In Europe, the war situation worsened. London suffered severe bombardments. And although we did not learn of it until later, in September of 1941 Hitler used poison gas at Auschwitz for the first time.

After the United States entered the war in December 1941, the rationing of gas, autos, tires, butter, meat, some other foods, and even shoes made civilian life more complicated. Filling the workplace void left by men who had entered military service, many women took jobs in factories, producing tanks, airplanes, and other items needed for the war effort. And in German-occupied France, women spies worked with the French underground movement and played a key role in helping the Allies ultimately achieve victory. When the War finally ended, 400,000 American servicemen had died.

A few of the songs that became popular during the War years were "The Last Time I Saw Paris," "How Are Things in Glocca Morra?"

"Sleepy Lagoon," and "The White Cliffs of Dover"—"There'll be blue-birds over the white cliffs of Dover, tomorrow, just you wait and see."

In 1939, the year *Gone with the Wind* was released, the average theater admission price was less than thirty cents. Often the admission would include two features, a newsreel, a cartoon, a travelogue, and sometimes even a stage show. My movie idol, Joseph Cotton, kept me enthralled with his roles in *Gaslight* (1944) with Ingrid Bergman and *Love Letters* (1945) with Jennifer Jones. I also adored Gregory Peck.

* * * *

EVEN THOUGH I DID WELL ACADEMICALLY, remaining on the honor roll throughout high school, and although my classmates had elected me to be on the student council each year and then class president during our senior year, I struggled with feelings of a lack of self-worth. Not until decades later would I begin to understand the reasons for this and feel more centered and confident in who I am. (*See* Chapter 14).

* * * *

MY INTEREST IN WRITING FOUND some expression through my being editor of our high school monthly newsletter, *The Buzzer*. The creative writing part was easy and fun, but the mechanical copying process of the periodical was often a nightmare.

Predating the development of photocopiers, we had to reproduce our periodical for circulation to fellow students on a mimeograph machine, one of Thomas Edison's inventions dating back to the 1880s. We couldn't simply insert a page of text into a machine and press a button to make copies. Cutting a stencil, correcting mistakes, inking the machine's cylindrical drum, and hand-cranking the machine were all laborious and extremely messy operations. While mimeograph machines are mostly obsolete, some college professors still prefer to use more up-to-date electric models for making copies of handouts for students.

* * * *

My oldest brother, Lt. Col. William Webster Dean (above), was a World War II torpedo bomber pilot in the South Pacific. At right, my brother Captain Sanford J. Dean, U.S. Army Signal Corps, World War II, 1943.

ALL THREE OF MY BROTHERS SERVED in the military during the 1940s. Bill was a Marine Air Corps torpedo bomber pilot flying combat missions in the South Pacific. Sandy was an officer in the Army Signal Corps in Europe. And my younger brother, John, served after the war with the occupation forces in Japan.

Sandy had a life-threatening accident in France. In 2004 I asked him to describe to me exactly what happened. Here is his story:

> I was in Paris, training a signal photo detachment of which I was the CO [Commanding Officer] when the Battle of the Bulge started. The German surge was threatening to overrun some of the area controlled by the Seventh Army. A Major and I and my driver were sent in my jeep to retrieve some equipment before it was overrun.
>
> We spent the night in Nancy, France, before going on to the front. We were billeted in a French villa, which had been taken over for an officers' quarters. I was sharing a ground floor room with another officer I had never met before. After dumping my

duffel bag, I asked him where the bathroom was. He said he didn't know, but why didn't I just step out into the garden as he had. There were some large French doors there. We were in a blackout so everything was pitch black. I opened the doors and stepped out— into space. I am not sure how far I fell, but it was quite deep, I would estimate at least fifteen feet to a sub-basement level, and, I think, a concrete floor. I pitched forward as I fell and landed on my upper body and the point of my chin crashed into the floor. I think I may have been briefly unconscious, but only briefly.

I became aware of some persons around me. I remember spitting out some teeth and putting my finger in my ear and commenting on the blood. A doc who was staying there was at my side and ordered me to keep my fingers out of my ear. I realized later that he recognized a fractured skull and he was fearful of infection. I vaguely remember being carried up a steep stairwell on a stretcher and not much more until the next day in the station hospital in Nancy. I remember the major and my driver coming into the ward and looking around, then walking out because they didn't recognize me with my badly swollen face.

I spent the next six weeks in the hospital. My jaw was wired shut. It had been broken in three places and I had a basal skull fracture. Several of my molars had been split in two by the blow. My right knee was injured and my left arm had a slight fracture. I got out of the hospital a little early because my unit had finished their training in Paris and were sent to the Seventh Army, and our initial location was in Nancy. I talked my way out and took over the unit there. I had been fitted with a partial upper plate in the hospital and I had extensive dental work years later in Minneapolis and in Syracuse, New York.

I always said that the skull fracture must have shaken up my brain for the good, because I was a so-so student before that time and when I returned from the Army I was a straight A student through my remaining undergrad and grad work, despite working twenty hours a week and carrying eighteen hours of courses. Who knows?"

Indeed! Sandy's lifetime career culminated in his serving for eighteen years as chair of the Department of Psychology at Northern Illinois University (NIU) in DeKalb, Illinois. He received in 2013 a Distinguished Faculty Award for his work as a key figure among the leaders who helped transform NIU from a small teaching college into the nationally recognized research university it has now become.

* * * *

THOUGH THE ANGUISH GENERATED by thinking about all the young boys being slaughtered in the War overseas haunted me daily, the summer following my Eden Prairie High School graduation in 1942 brought tragedy close to home. Two of my classmates—Chester Teich and George Shorba—owned motorcycles. Cyclists in those days didn't wear safety helmets. George Shorba, the shy son of immigrant parents, died instantly after being flung from his motorcycle on striking at high speed the concrete abutment of an overpass at a sharp turn in a country road in Eden Prairie township. Seeing him so still and white, lying in a coffin in the mortuary, was a shock to me, making me even physically sick. A young life snuffed out so suddenly, so needlessly. It was hard to believe and accept. My high school experience ended with this tragedy.

Me on the day after my high school graduation, 1942.

Chapter 6

Courtship by Correspondence

B ILL HAD OFFERED TO PAY MY TU-
ITION to attend business college.
So after graduating from high
school in June 1942, I enrolled in a secretarial finishing course at the Minneapolis Business College. My social life
consisted of infrequent dates with civilian men classified as 4-F by the military
because of some physical impairment.
But in 1943 I met and began dating an
interesting Army Air Force serviceman.
Some church friends of our family—the
Wintersteins—invited me to a party they
were giving for servicemen stationed at
the University of Minnesota. Among the
guys stood a tall, blonde, shy, good-look-
ing Air Force serviceman named Ernest
Breton.

"Hi, there, I'm Ernie. Okay if I sit
here next to you?"

"Uh, um, sure. What are you
doing at the university?"

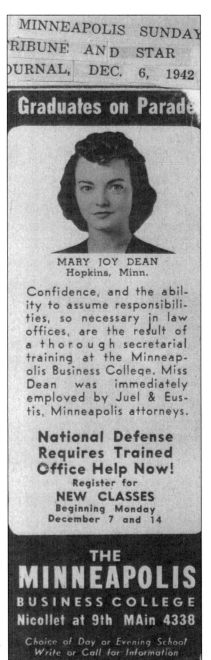

MINNEAPOLIS SUNDAY
TRIBUNE AND STAR
JURNAL, DEC. 6, 1942

Graduates on Parade

MARY JOY DEAN
Hopkins, Minn.

Confidence, and the abil-
ity to assume responsibilities, so necessary in law
offices, are the result of
a thorough secretarial
training at the Minneap-
olis Business College. Miss
Dean was immediately
employed by Juel & Eus-
tis, Minneapolis attorneys.

**National Defense
Requires Trained
Office Help Now!**
Register for
NEW CLASSES
Beginning Monday
December 7 and 14

**THE
MINNEAPOLIS
BUSINESS COLLEGE
Nicollet at 9th MAin 4338**
*Choice of Day or Evening School
Write or Call for Information*

Minneapolis Business College advertisement featuring me.

"Well I'm in a meteorology program preparing for Officers' Candidate School (OCS). Like most guys, I wanted to be a pilot, but I'm colorblind and that disqualified me." Ernie asked me about my life and my job. We talked throughout the evening. As we stood to leave, his six-foot frame towered over my five-foot-two.

"Can I see you again?" Thus began a serious relationship. I was living with my Aunt Rachel and Grandmother Lydia Ann Webster Armstrong, sleeping on a cot in the dining room of their Hennepin Avenue apartment in Minneapolis. Ernie rode the trolley from the university to come visit. Our dates often consisted of strolls along the nearby Lake of the Isles, usually ending with a chocolate sundae at Bridgeman's. Sometimes, when weekend leaves allowed, he went with me to my Eden

Lt. Ernest J. Breton writing to me from the South Pacific, World War II.

Prairie dwelling for some home cooking. He quickly won the hearts of my family.

In November 1943, the Air Force transferred Ernie to Connecticut to attend Officer Candidate School (OCS). Except for a couple brief leaves—during one of which we traveled by train to visit his family—we had no further time together before he was shipped to the South Pacific. For the remainder of World War II, our courtship consisted of letters to each other.

In the meantime, after finishing business college late in 1942, I worked first for Juel & Eustis, divorce lawyers in the Foshay Tower in Minneapolis. But they lacked sufficient cases to justify my employment. Then I worked briefly for Anchor Casualty, an insurance claim agency. My situation after that in the Dean of Students' Office at the University of Minnesota proved to be a longer lasting, challenging, and fun job. My boss, the assistant dean and disciplinary counselor, also functioned as foreign student advisor. Because his disciplinary responsibilities demanded most of his time and attention, the counseling of foreign students fell largely to me. This gave me the opportunity to meet and help students who needed assistance in adjusting to being far from home and lonely in a strange culture.

One student from Pakistan, Irshad Nabi Mien, came into the office frequently. He seemed especially forlorn. Sometimes I invited him to visit my family and share a meal with us. One time he volunteered to prepare a Pakistani rice dish as part of our meal. He used up our week's worth of rationed butter, but it was delicious.

Irshad knew I was in a committed relationship with Ernie Breton, but nevertheless he wrote two touching love letters to me.

During the three years I worked in the Dean of Students Office at the university, Dimitri Mitropoulis was the permanent conductor of the Minneapolis Symphony Orchestra. The concerts I attended in Northrup Auditorium remain in my memory as peak experiences.

On weekends I sometimes rode the Greyhound bus home from Minneapolis to Eden Prairie. One time, while standing near the driver on an overcrowded bus, I smelled rubber burning. Another young woman next to me noticed it also. We told the driver and he pulled the

Ernie's and my garden wedding, August 31, 1946.

bus off the highway to investigate. The bus had to be evacuated as it was on fire. A feature story, including photos about the event appeared in the June 24, 1945, *Minneapolis Morning Tribune*."[5]

In 1945, the nation mourned President Franklin D. Roosevelt's death, and on that day I received a package from Ernie's mother. He had asked her to select for him and send to me a diamond engagement ring. And so on a windy day at the end of August 1946, we married under an arched rose trellis in our Eden Prairie garden. Gloria, a colleague of mine in the Dean of Students' Office, provided harp music for the event. Another co-worker, a Japanese-American long-time friend and skilled seamstress, created several pieces of clothing for my trousseau.

Following our garden wedding and reception, Ernie and I piled our luggage into our first car—an old Hudson—and headed for Minnesota's North Shore for what I had envisioned to be an idyllic honeymoon.

"[5]Girls Smell Smoke, Give First Warning," Minneapolis Morning Tribune, June 24, 1945.

"Where will we be staying tonight?" Ernie wanted to know.

"Well, uh, I don't know. I guess we'll have to look for a place."

If I had it to do over again, I would make wedding night reservations at a modern hotel in Minneapolis. At the time, though, I thought we could just discover some comfortable accommodations along the way as we drove toward Duluth. But in 1946, Minnesota north of the Twin Cities was not yet developed to serve tourists. After driving about fifty miles northward and with darkness approaching, we came to Princeton,

Ernie and me, 1947.

a small town where the population, even as recently as the 2000 census, numbered fewer than 5,000 people.

We found the one hotel in Princeton to be a shabby old wooden structure that had been converted from some previous purpose.

"I guess this will have to do," Ernie whispered as he signed the guest register. Our sparsely furnished small room reeked of stale tobacco. No private bathroom either, only a shared lavatory at the end of a long hall with creaky floorboards. Through the thin walls we could hear the raucous voices of guests on either side. No romantic ambience here.

Approaching Duluth the next afternoon, we checked out available lodgings . . . nothing but rows of primitive cottages without heat, running water, or indoor plumbing. Ernie had to use a pulley and bucket system to dip water from Lake Superior for washing. He was a better sport about it than I was, as he didn't seem to mind all this "roughing it." But I had had my fill of living under such conditions in Eden Prairie during the Great Depression in the 1930s, and the experience hardly reflected my idea of a honeymoon. Nevertheless, my own lack of planning was responsible.

After a few days of this, we decided to abandon the North Shore idea and head back to the Twin Cities and a hot shower. A few days later, we left for Florida. This trip proved to be pleasant with modern motels every night all along the way.

Being an unseasoned traveler, I made the mistake of packing my clothes in several different suitcases by category—the same way I stored them in my dresser—underclothes in one suitcase, dresses in another, and so forth. Ernie, after a couple nights of lugging in my several suitcases ventured, "Do you think you could put all your overnight stuff in just one suitcase?"

Chapter 7

Working toward My "P.H.T." Degree

WHEN PRESIDENT FRANKLIN D. ROOSEVELT signed the G.I. Bill of Rights Act in 1944, more than a year before World War II ended, he made higher education available to millions of veterans, including my husband, Ernie. The government paid for college tuition fees and books plus a small monthly subsistence allowance, in our case about $100.

Before being drafted into military service in 1942, Ernie had completed a year of college at Auburn University in Alabama. While waiting for admission in 1947 to the Missouri School of Mines and Metallurgy in Rolla, Missouri, to resume his college education, we worked during the first six months of our marriage in Breton's Coffee Shop, a soda fountain/restaurant his parents had established in Winter Haven, Florida. His mother, an outstanding cook herself, planned the menus and supervised the kitchen employees. I typed up the daily menus and waited on tables. Ernie assumed responsibility for much of the general management. His father manned the cash register. A mining engineer by profession with no public relations sensitivity, Ernie's Dad sometimes told off the customers (mostly retired folks) if they complained about the food or service while paying their check: "If you weren't so damn lazy, you'd go home and cook dinner yourselves." We wondered if they would ever come back, but eventually they did. Breton's Coffee Shop had a reputation in town for great food.

During our sojourn in Rolla, Missouri, while Ernie attended classes, I created a public stenographic service to supplement his GI subsistence, sharing an office with an electrical contractor. Graduate students engaged me to edit and type their Master's theses and Doctoral dissertations on my manual typewriter.

Ernie's selection of metallurgy as his major kept his focus on science courses—chemistry, physics, math, and engineering. He had little interest in liberal arts courses. One day he handed me a 500-page English literature anthology.

"Here, this is a required course. How about reading my assignments as we go along and telling me about them? I don't have time."

So I did. Ernie received an "A" in the course and never cracked the book. In hindsight, this probably was an unethical thing for me to do. But being a product of the post World War II cultural conditioning of veterans' wives, it just seemed part of my role to "put hubby through."

We lived in several different furnished one-room apartments during our years in Rolla, the first one a basement apartment that flooded during a Missouri cloudburst. A storm drain outside had become plugged up. I had been serving as "Second Reader" in the local Christian Science Church, and Ernie and I came home after church one Sunday in 1948 to six inches of water in our apartment. While Ernie worked outside to stanch the flow of water, I rushed about inside lifting our belongings up out of the water. I made the mistake of grabbing a metal floor lamp while standing in the water and suffered an intense electrical shock that sent me to the edge of the beyond. I fell, unconscious into the water on the floor, clutching the lamp stand which fell across my face, burning a streak. A British friend, Philippa Calkins, whom I had telephoned to come help us clean up the mess, arrived just as I screamed. She had driven an ambulance during the London Blitz and had picked up many casualties. She shouted to Ernie to turn off the power. Then she checked me out. No pulse, no breathing. Her husband, Bob, picked me up and put me on the bed. Then, to the best of their ability, Phil and Ernie applied their understanding of Christian Science metaphysical healing to the situation. Eventually, after what Ernie characterized as an interminable length of time, actually perhaps about five minutes, I gasped, took a breath, frothed at the mouth, then after a long pause, took another breath. They carried me to Phil's house and had to cut my wet clothes off because I struggled against them so fiercely. I remained unconscious for twenty-four hours. When I regained consciousness I could remember nothing of what had happened.

In July 1949, our first daughter, Leslie, joined us. Around 3:00 a.m. on July 21, I began having regular contractions. I awakened Ernie to alert him. And I called the doctor. But knowing this was my first pregnancy, the doctor said, "Relax. Nothing's going to happen until tomorrow afternoon."

I believed otherwise. The contractions continued to become more frequent. The nearest hospital, previously an Army hospital at Fort Leonard Wood, Missouri, meant a thirty-mile drive from Rolla. This made me nervous.

So in the wee hours of the morning, while I continued timing contractions, trying to decide when to depart for the hospital, Ernie entertained himself reading Thucydides' *History of the Peloponnesian War*, a struggle in ancient Greece! The contractions steadily became more frequent. Around 4:30 or 5:00 a.m. I said, "Come on, Ernie, let's get to the hospital."

My hair, all done up in my usual night-time pin curls and covered with a kerchief, stayed that way throughout the prep and delivery process. I wanted my hair to look nice after the baby's birth. But perspiration generated by the July heat and the birth process turned my hair sour. I had never been in a hospital before and was unfamiliar with hospital routines and pre-delivery procedures. Our daughter, Leslie, arrived around 9:00 a.m. The doctor must have had to break the speed limit to arrive in time.

After Ernie obtained his Master's Degree in metallurgy in 1950 at the Missouri School of Mines and Metallurgy, he accepted a position in sales with a chemical company in Philadelphia. But within only a few months, he realized that research, not sales, drew his greatest interest. We returned to Florida to help manage the family Coffee Shop once again, while contemplating our next options.

When the Army Air Force discharged Ernie after World War II, they had persuaded him to sign up as a Reserve Officer for a five-year enlistment. Their argument: "How could there possibly be another war in five years?" But they were wrong. The Air Force recalled Ernie to active duty when the Korean War broke out in June of 1950, only a few months before his five-year re-enlistment would have ended. He had never attended any Reserve Officers' events; and because we had moved several times, the Air Force couldn't find him. At one point they declared him AWOL. The active duty orders finally caught up with us in Florida, assigning him to a post in Alaska. However, because of his Masters Degree in metallurgy, the Air Force decided to assign him instead to do titanium research at the Wright Patterson Air Force Base in Dayton, Ohio.

So for eighteen months we made our home in a second-floor apartment of a large old house on King Street in the small Ohio town of Xenia near Dayton. Television had become popular, so we bought a used set. Of course, it was black and white. But we found the early TV shows highly entertaining: Arthur Godfrey, Red Skelton, Jack Benny, and the Fireside Theatre productions.

On Ernie's final discharge from the Air Force, this time for good, we once again shuttled back to Florida. Ernie had decided to seek a Ph.D. in physical chemistry at the University of Florida in Gainesville.

Chapter 8

Tears and Triumphs of the 1950s

MOST DAYS ERNIE RODE HIS MOTOR scooter to the University of Florida campus in Gainesville where he sought a Ph.D. in physical chemistry and worked as a teaching assistant. At home, I resumed my public stenographic services for graduate students to supplement our meager income. As well, I created all my own and the children's clothes and even some of Ernie's and cooked hamburger and tuna fish casseroles to save money.

On November 1, 1953, our second daughter, Denise, arrived. When she was less than three months old, on January 30, 1954, my father called me from Minnesota. He was crying. "I have tragic news. William died today in a plane crash in Massachusetts."

Stunned, I collapsed to the floor. How could this be? A skilled pilot—a highly decorated Lieutenant Colonel in the Marine Air Corps—he had flown a torpedo bomber through more than a thousand hours of dangerous combat in the South Pacific, being the first to land any kind of airplane on the hard-won Iwo Jima Island.

"What happened?"

"He was caught in a violent snow squall near Concord, Massachusetts, while returning from Canada. When he was only fifteen minutes flying time from his destination, the plane went out of control."

Through an open window I heard the cooing of a mourning dove. It was too much.

After the war, Bill had completed college, then partnered with the founder of Helio Aircraft Corporation in Massachusetts. In the little startup business, he wore numerous hats, including business manager, test pilot, and salesman. Pre-dating the invention of jet airplanes, the "Helio Courier," a new airplane design known nationally for its safety, featured an outsized propeller making it possible to land on short runways at speeds as low as twenty-seven miles an hour. Bill had flown the plane to Canada to demonstrate it to a potential buyer.

"Yesterday I was restless with an intuition that something ominous was about to happen involving William," my father added. "I should have acted on it."

I wanted the whole world to back up in time so we could relive that horrible day and prevent this devastating accident. How could everyone around us continue to go about business as usual as though nothing had happened? Didn't they know?

My grieving days were consumed with home management, typing dissertations, sewing and caring for Denise, our new baby girl, and her older sister, Leslie. We also often entertained foreign students from the university, learning about different cultures. The activities kept me busy, but inside I felt numb.

* My brother Bill beside "Helio Courier" in 1953.

FLORIDA'S CLIMATE FOSTERED THE YEAR-ROUND popularity of drive-in theaters. Occasionally after bedding down our two small girls, Leslie and Denise, in the tailgate of our Chevy station wagon, we'd head for a drive-in, the one indulgence we could afford. A number of 1950s actors and films still stand out in my memory. Among them are Spencer Tracy in *Bad Day at Black Rock*, Cary Grant and Grace Kelly in *To Catch a Thief*, Burt Lancaster and Deborah Kerr in *From Here to Eternity*, and *Around the World in 80 Days*, starring British actor David Niven.

By January 1957, Ernie had obtained his doctorate and accepted a research position with DuPont in Wilmington, Delaware. During our four years in Gainesville, we had been able to save $1,000. Ernie's $9,600 starting salary at DuPont seemed like a fortune to us at the time.

As a 1957 Christmas gift and to express his gratitude to me for my ten years of "Putting Hubby Through," Ernie bought a Conn spinet organ for me, truly my P.H.T. degree. I had hours of enjoyment teaching myself to play.

Our third and last little girl, Jeannine, came on income tax day, April 15, 1961. Exactly one month later, I stood at a table in front of the television set changing her diaper as the Freedom 7 spaceship with Alan Shepherd aboard shot into its fifteen-minute sub-orbital flight. The decade had been life-changing for me and the world as well.

Chapter 9

More about My Parents

My mother on her eightieth birthday, wearing the dress she hand-sewed, showing the tumbling spray of flowers she textile-painted on the dress.

MY MOTHER CONTINUED TO PAINT in watercolor, oil, pastel, acrylic late into her life. She even decorated a dress she sewed for herself with a spray of pink flowers. She also made and sold placemats and napkins as well as notecards decorated with flowers. She had applied her artistic talents to build our family's income during the Great Depression, and our survival was largely due to her resourcefulness, frugality, creativity, courage, management skills, and gut-grinding hard work. She had created a small business, eventually adding on a flower and gourd shop to the front corner of our Eden Prairie home. She gained regional renown as "the gourd lady."

After my father retired from Minneapolis Moline at age seventy-five, my parents escaped the Minnesota winters by relocating to Winter Haven, Florida. For a number of years, my mother conducted art classes in their home—mainly for children, some from disadvantaged families and families of color. One artistically talented young man of color whom she coached went on to attend an art college, earned his degree, and obtained a job as a commercial artist.

My mother had many admirable qualities and many people loved her. But she also suffered from what therapists now describe as wounds to her psyche, which stemmed from traumas in her childhood. And, of course, she reflected the social conditioning of her generation.

The death of her father when she was only four years old took a physical and emotional toll on her. Her grieving mother, Lydia Ann Webster Armstrong, never a very demonstrative person, withdrew emotionally in her sorrow and was unable to provide the affection and nurturing reassurances that my mother needed.

When my grandmother traveled to California to seek healing, she left the children in the care of neighbors. This compounded my mother's feeling of abandonment. When my grandmother returned to the family farm near Arlington, South Dakota, several weeks later, she relied on her growing understanding of Christian Science and the healing prayers of Christian Science practitioners to deal with her children's illnesses. Considering that the medical help of the day had likely caused my grandfather's death, neither my grandmother nor her children trusted medical help. But neighbors often ridiculed her for her beliefs—sometimes even intervening—especially when my grandmother failed to seek medical help for my sickly mother.

When my mother had children of her own, she undoubtedly wanted to be the exemplary parent she as a child longed for and had experienced in her father. She strove for a perfect and harmonious family of well-behaved children free of what she termed "discord"—children who never quarreled or expressed anger. And having been deprived of sufficient demonstrations of affection by her mother, she bent over backwards to give her children physical affection.

But each child is different, and for me, her expressions of motherly concern felt smothering and made me want to withdraw. Somewhere along the way, I lost touch with my feelings, pulled back, and numbed out.

My mother, a slight person no more than five feet tall, had hazel eyes and brown hair. During the years she wore her hair long, she crimped it by twisting and winding sections each night around six wide metal hair barrettes. She wore glasses with thick lenses. Early in mid-life, she developed osteoporosis. Her back looked like a question mark. In my ignorance, I thought she just had bad posture and encouraged her to try to stand up straight. She said her hump resulted from her having to scrub floors as a child and that she had the "Haskell Hump," noting that it ran in the family, dating back at least to my great grand-mother, Mercy Haskell Herring Webster.

My mother suffered from frequent migraine headaches, which were often brought on by the slightest squabbling among us siblings. While she lacked self-assurance as a child and young woman, my mother be-came more controlling as the years went by. Her bond with Christian Science also took her toward self-righteousness. And she was a perfec-tionist for herself and us. Her love was conditional: "If you love me, you will do (or won't do) x." I had to behave according to the standards she had set for "Mary's little Joy." As I said, expressing anger was a no-no. Even thinking bad thoughts was "sinful."

She never spanked us, but she used shame to control us. "Aren't you ashamed of yourself? You're letting naughty thoughts talk to you." Emotional manipulation was her method for maintaining a "peaceful family," which was her highest priority. I learned early on to be exces-sively obedient and "good" to ensure her love. Of course, the price was stuffing my real emotions.

Reflecting the social conditioning of her generation, my mother be-lieved sex was exclusively for having babies. As I matured, she often lec-tured me about being aware of men's sinful intentions.

She also bossed my British-born father, even forbidding him to drink tea and coffee—a British man not allowed to have afternoon tea in his own home! She considered tea and coffee habit-forming and therefore sinful. During the mid-1960s, my parents lived with my family and me in Delaware for over a year when my mother was seriously ill and bed-ridden.

During that time, I cooked for seven people, while giving my mother nursing care and managing the household. It was a stressful period. But I often took time to make afternoon tea for my Cornish father. It was our secret.

Trying to compel me to agree with her views or positions, she would end her espousals by asking, "Don't you say so?" She put me in an awkward and uncomfortable spot, because often I didn't "say so." She also tried to control my grown daughters. Denise was breaking away from the Christian Science church to pursue independent spiritual study. My mother was absolutely opposed: "If you love me, you won't do that." Denise did it anyway, and I did as well. But my mother scarcely spoke with Denise ever again, showing her disapproval in many subtle and not so subtle facial expressions and in giving her "silent treatment." Denise visited her and made overtures in an effort to heal the breach, but to no avail. Even at holidays, she refused to speak to Denise or even acknowledge her greeting or presence. This was hard to watch or fathom.

After my father passed on, my mother sold their home in Florida and relocated to an apartment in Wilmington, Delaware, near where our family was living at the time. Our pre-teen youngest daughter, Jeannine, often stayed with my mother on the occasional weekends when Ernie and I holidayed in New York City. Jeannine hit it off with her: "We cooked together, made chocolate milk shakes and popcorn, did grocery shopping. Grandma's stories triggered my enduring interest in gardening, especially in growing gourds, in collecting rocks and seashells, in antiques, and in our family's history."

When my mother, in her nineties, moved back to Minneapolis, Jeannine, newly relocated to the Twin Cities as well, shared an apartment with her for about a year. "The first six months were fun," Jeannine recalls, "but, then Grandma began invading my boundaries, snooping in my personal business, criticizing me for making long-distance calls (which I paid for), or for buying clothes I needed to wear to work, or complaining about Lolie, my cat." Now a strong woman, Jeannine stood up to my mother when she used tears as a means to manipulate her: "Don't pull that stuff on me!"

I stopped idealizing my mother when I married, but it wasn't until twenty-five or thirty years later (in the 1960s and 1970s) that I consciously faced up to her patterns more objectively. I began to understand how her controlling behavior was her coping response to her own dysfunctional family and traumatic childhood.

Ten years after my mother died, my brother, John, told me that he felt he had had an unfulfilling life with failed trucking ventures and two unhappy marriages. "As you know," John reminded me, "Uncle Fremont [our mother's younger brother] had a flourishing greenhouse business in Chelsea, Michigan. After World War II, he wanted me to come to Michigan to work with him and eventually take over the business." Uncle Fremont had no children. John had always loved gardening and horticulture. He wanted to pursue this opportunity. But our mother pressured him not to go but to stay in Minnesota near her, saying she "needed him." In other words, "If you love me, you won't do that." John regretted that he allowed our mother to pressure him about such a critical life decision and deprive him of a lucrative career and a fulfilling occupation.

My mother passed on at age ninety-five in a Christian Science nursing home in Minneapolis. I seldom remember dreams, but I clearly recall one I had a few months after she died. In my dream, she sat in an armchair on a raised platform. Her eyes, huge and glowing—looked like gold-colored balls of fire. In actual fact, she had rather small eyes. With her intensely glowing eyes in the dream fixed on me, I felt absolutely frozen, paralyzed by her stare, unable to move or escape from the spell of it.

But while this dream described the emotional paralysis I felt, I continued with my own development. In the early 1990s, I began exploring various spiritual traditions. Still working in Manhattan, I read Michael Harner's book, *The Way of the Shaman*, twice. The work drew me, so when Michael Harner gave a weekend workshop at the Omega Institute of Holistic Studies in Rhinebeck, New York, I took the scenic train-ride along the Hudson River up to Rhinebeck to attend. During an inner meditational journey that weekend, I went to an inner realm that many describe as the "upper world," and my mother appeared to me. She was crying and told me she was sorry about many things and hoped I would forgive her. Her message touched me, and the experience brought peace about my often-conflicted relationship with her.

*   *   *   *

My father made up in a warm, deep, and resonant voice what he lacked in physical stature. He educated himself by becoming a voracious reader. Lacking a formal education, though, he had to learn a trade—paper-hanging and painting—as an occupation.

He adored us children, having waited until he was forty to marry and have a family. He spent a great deal of time playing with us and reading to us. Then came the Great Depression. My father was devastated by what he perceived as his colossal failure to support the family he cherished and had found so late in life. Frustration, a collapsing sense of self-worth, and despair left him emotionally drained. He continued to read to us and tried to play games, but it was obvious that he was depressed and his thoughts were elsewhere. I think this is why my mother took charge of the family. She needed to hold things together when everything was falling apart, but she pushed it into a habit of dominating my father, even treating him like a child. She set the family rules and kept the pace rolling, and my father learned to accept a subordinate role in the relationship. He apparently agreed with her philosophy about sex or at least went along with it. Years later, he lectured two of his small granddaughters (then only seven and eleven or so) about the evils of sex. At the time, they had no clue what he was talking about.

My brother Sandy—a Ph.D. psychologist and retired university professor and department chairman—remains a social liberal who has voted mostly, but not exclusively, Democratic tickets. He and I found our father's political alliance baffling. Even though my father's job with the WPA, created under President Franklin D. Roosevelt, sustained our family during the Great Depression, and notwithstanding his being heavily dependent on Social Security in later life (which the Republicans had opposed and tried to kill), he remained a staunch Republican, voting consistently against his own best interests.

During the 1950s, Sandy engaged in some hot political arguments with our father. Like many of us, Sandy was outraged by the witch-hunts of Senator Joseph McCarthy, which were destroying many innocent people's lives. But Dad regarded McCarthy as a patriot and envisioned communists "everywhere under the bed," as Sandy put it. "If you don't like it here, perhaps you should go live in Russia," Dad suggested. It sounded as though Dad thought Sandy was a communist sympathizer, which was not Sandy's position at all.

Speculating on why Dad voted as he did, Sandy surmises it was his desire to identify with the upper class and his belief that Republicans were somehow the more moral people. Sandy thinks Dad also believed the "enemy Catholics" controlled the Democratic Party. Sandy recalls Dad being convinced that Al Smith (the four-term New York State Governor, a Catholic and Democratic presidential nominee in 1928 opposing Herbert Hoover) was the emissary of the pope. Dad believed that if Al Smith had been elected president, the pope would have been running the country. Of course, that was the Republican doctrine of the time. Sandy recalls Dad cautioning him to beware of Catholic girls—that the Catholic Church encouraged Catholic girls to marry Protestant boys to bring them into the church, thus increasing the number of Catholics. The sad thing is that such views were common in the United States during the period.

I love my parents, and years have helped me understand why they behaved as they did. My father was rather a proud person, though not without humility. He was kind, refined, and dignified, which made the misfortunes that so many men of his generation faced all the more painful for him. And my mother was a survivor. Because of her, we made it through. When the urge to control was not getting the better of her, she modeled qualities of resourcefulness and perseverance in truly scary circumstances that, throughout my life, have given me strength and focus in difficult times.

Chapter 10

Pungent Pennsylvania

T HE PUNGENT STENCH OF HORSE MANURE jolted us awake the morning after we moved into the house we had bought in Southeastern Chester County, Pennsylvania. Where was the foul odor coming from?

When Ernie accepted DuPont's job offer early in 1957, we sought out a realtor to show us some housing options in or near Wilmington, Delaware. Ernie's future boss at DuPont recommended a realtor—an elder in a Presbyterian church in nearby Kennett Square, Pennsylvania.

Of the several choices the realtor showed us, Ernie favored a two-story farmhouse set close to Highway 1 near West Grove, Pennsylvania, not far over the Delaware border and just a few miles from Longwood Gardens near Kennett Square. Two narrow acres of land stretched over a rise behind the house leading into a deep horseshoe-shaped glen set in a cliff that had once been a limestone quarry several decades earlier. The glen, with the cliffs now forested, captured Ernie's enthusiasm. I was less than charmed by the house, but we bought the place anyway.

The realtor failed to tell us that Southeastern Chester County held the distinction of being the mushroom-growing capitol of the world, and our house sat smack in the middle of this activity. In fact, directly across the highway from our house, a massive, steaming horse-manure composting operation serving the region's mushroom growers spread over most of the valley. And we learned that our next-door neighbor was a mushroom grower.

When the realtor had shown us the property several months earlier, the two brothers/partners of the composting enterprise had been feuding, shutting the business down (along with the odor) temporarily. The realtor neglected to tell us about the business across the highway.

We felt like ignorant, greenhorn suckers from Florida, stuck with a raw deal. What to do? Nothing much we could do but make the best of it. The house badly needed some basic improvements. We insulated the attic, converted the coal furnace to an automatic oil burner and installed a hot-water heater along with a clothes washer and dryer. We also redecorated the kitchen and the bathroom. At the same time, I made the rounds of junk shops, collecting additional pieces of old furniture and refinishing them. In the process, I learned how to cane and rush chair seats. On the side I wrote short articles that were published in *The Christian Science Monitor*.

Often we invited foreign students attending nearby Lincoln University to come for dinner, and their visits proved to be enriching experiences for the family. Students from Korea, Ghana, and Greece often joined us for cookouts in our glen or for holiday meals. The students shared stories about their cultures and families. The student from Korea became a long-time friend. He showered us with handcrafted gifts made by his family, including a silk-embroidered image of a young girl playing an oriental musical instrument, and a half-gourd wall hanging decorated with a hand painted scene of a Korean pipe ceremony. He also gave us two scrolls of Korean calligraphy. I framed them using monk's cloth-covered cardboard for mats. Almost fifty years later they still hang in our St. Paul, Minnesota, living room, often serving as conversation pieces among guests.

Ernie disliked mowing the lawn, preferring to spend his weekends reading trade journals, such as *Chemical & Engineering News*. His solution? Buy a couple goats. Recalling tales my grandmother and my Uncle Fremont told me about the behavior and habits of Billy goats, I was dubious. But Ernie pursued the idea. We ended up with two just-weaned white female kids—one a Nubian and the other a Saanen breed.

Truly endearing creatures, they climbed into our laps, nibbled at our ears or pencils in our pockets, slipped through the back door into the kitchen.

Lerslie and Denise with nanny goat kids, behind our house near West Grove, Pennsylvania, 1959.

Did they eat our grass as Ernie hoped? No. They preferred to defoliate our newly planted Japanese maple sapling, our weigela, and other ornamental shrubs. When we offered them treats such as carrot peelings served up in a Kleenex box, they ate the box first.

In the beginning we housed them in a makeshift pen in our garage. Then we tried tethering them to trees. While Ernie was at work and the girls in school, it fell to me to unwind the goats from the trees and refill their kicked-over water buckets. Then Ernie tried tethering them to leashes attached to a helix stake. But they easily pulled the helix stakes up.

Ernie's next approach to corralling the goats involved enclosing them in an electric fenced area. They easily slithered under the fence. Ernie wired an antennae to the one goat with horns. But they then vaulted right over the top. Outfitting them with collars and a dangling chain to connect them to a shock didn't work either. Ernie's stack of trade journals languished while he spent weekends trying to outsmart the goats.

With the approach of fall, Ernie built a floorless shed set on skids made of two-by-fours. The shed, constructed from homosote, a fiberboard made from old newspapers and waste cardboard, could just be dragged around our apple orchard, organically fertilizing the trees while eliminating any need for mucking out their quarters.

The goats loved the shed. They ate it up. As holes appeared in the sides, Ernie spent his weekends squaring them up into windows and covering them with hardware cloth. The goats would butt Ernie's backsides rhythmically as he worked away at sawing the holes into windows. Once Ernie matched their rocking motion, they jumped aside, bleating their pleasure as Ernie fell backwards into the mud.

One hole after another appeared in the shed. The goats were literally eating themselves out of house and home. One morning in mid-April we looked out the kitchen window to see one of the goat's heads sticking out through a hole they had eaten in the shed's roof. The goats had outfoxed Ernie at every turn. The weekend hours he had devoted to dealing with their capricious behavior far exceeded the time mowing the lawn would have required. Further research revealed that browsing goats are best at clipping back tough or poisonous weeds, twigs, or shrubs and that they eat grass *last of all*. Ernie conceded defeat. We found a goat farmer who was happy to buy the goats.

The winter of 1957–1958 was reported to be the worst winter in Pennsylvania in over forty years. A February blizzard closed schools for a week. Then on March 20–21 (the first days of spring) three feet of wet, heavy snow brought down power lines and poles, leaving residents without power for three days. The power and telephone companies worked with capacity crews to reinstate service. They flew men in by helicopter because the snow prevented them from reaching the breakdown areas by truck.

Without electricity, we were stuck. The water to the house was pumped with an electric pump; our stove was electric; our oil furnace was run by an electric motor; and we had no outhouse anymore. Chilled to the bone and snowbound, we layered on multiple garments. As soon as darkness fell, there was nothing to do but go to bed.

We tried heating food with candles, but it was slow and sooty. Finally, Ernie waded out to the garage in hip-deep snow to fetch his blowtorch. Hot chocolate never tasted so good. But how to wash the dishes without water? We tried melting snow for this and for flushing the toilet, but the house was so cold the snow wouldn't melt. The dishes just stacked up in the sink.

On the third day, we were able to hire a man to plow out our driveway. Ernie discovered that the roof of the garage had caved in under the snow's weight, slightly denting our car. But the next morning (a Saturday), we packed a suitcase of clean clothes and towels and abandoned the house. We all took hot showers in the men's locker room at the DuPont Experimental Station, savored a hot meal at Howard Johnson's, and then went to see the movie *The King and I*.

As we approached West Grove on our way home, we saw our house lights on and cheered.

The experience caused us to make preparations for future emergencies by obtaining a lantern, a camp stove, a transistor radio, and canned food reserves.

After living in the mushroom-composting neighborhood for over two years, I prevailed on Ernie to sell the house and relocate. We decided to engage the same broker to resell the house who had sold it to us. We insisted that he tell any potential buyer about the composting operation across the highway from the property.

"You'll never sell it," he said.

"Well," we insisted, "you try. And if you don't tell the buyer, we will." Before long, he *did* sell the house, and this time with full disclosure.

Chapter 11

Marriage

FOR CENTURIES, WOMEN IN MANY CULTURES, certainly European-based, have been taught that they should not be self-assertive—that men didn't like it. Rather, we should be submissive, subservient, subsumed, agreeable, supportive, sexually responsive on signal, and not too smart. We should also accept the opinions and attitudes of men as law, always bending to their wishes. In other words, we have been programmed to play the female role of yielding to patriarchy.

Because of this indoctrination, women have been stuck with most of the grunt work involved in daily living—dirty clothes, dirty dishes, dirty diapers, dirty houses, dirty toilets, leading to a life of servitude.

Fifty years into my life and nearly thirty years into my marriage, it dawned on me that lack of self-assertiveness had locked me into frustrating life circumstances, and that gender-role patterns are difficult to change. I discovered it is easy to lose one's identify, become smothered in the shadow of another and regarded as little more than someone's wife or mother.

I was a product of this prevalent cultural conditioning. During my children's growing-up years, I accepted the traditional role of women as my fate in life. But after thirty years of doing all the stereotypical jobs expected of wives—plus some less-expected jobs of being my spouse's barber, editor, and clerk typist—I began to rebel.

Home managers (a more accurate characterization than "house-wives") never receive a salary. However, their individual contributions to the nation's gross domestic product (GDP)—totally overlooked by the government—has been estimated to range from at least $25,000 to over

$100,000 a year per woman, all things considered (love and devotion not counted). The job includes being: nursemaid; childrearing specialist; housekeeper/cleaner; cook; dishwasher; laundress; food buyer and inventory keeper; chauffeur; gardener; maintenance person; seamstress; dietician; practical nurse; home decorator; and budget manager. According to the UN Development Fund for Women and World Bank surveys, "Women perform sixty-six percent of the world's work, produce fifty percent of the food, but earn ten percent of the income and own one percent[6] of the property." First unconsciously and then more consciously, I came to my limit on tolerating such circumstances.

So, when an unsolicited career opportunity—salaried even—came my way in the late 1960s, I seized it. In the end, my returning to the work world for the next twenty-seven years allowed me to have a comfortable retirement income, independent of any spousal support. If I hadn't returned to the work world, I suspect I might very well be destitute today and without a home of my own and pension income.

* * * *

PERHAPS I AM A MORE PRIVATE PERSON than many women, I enjoy being by myself. My idea of an ideal living arrangement with a spouse would have been to have my own private suite either under the same roof or under a separate one. And as a light sleeper, I personally prefer to have a bed all to myself. Of course, most newly married couples cannot afford the luxury of such space. Many families here and across the world live in crowded living conditions because of poverty, as my family did after the Depression hit. I had lived with six people to one room, and the idea of having my own living space seemed like a dream to me.

Because at mid-life I had not yet learned that it was okay for a woman to be self-assertive and to have personal boundaries, I had allowed gross daily intrusions of my privacy—even bathroom privacy. My

UN Development Fund for Women and World Bank Surveys, "Women, Business and the Law," 2012, Foreword, p. 1.

husband once said the test of true love was seeing your spouse on the john. I came to realize I could no longer keep passing that test.

The daily witnessing of personal habits can erode a love relationship, at least it did for me. I agree with film actor Omar Sharif, who once said in an interview that annoying personal habits can be overlooked early in a love relationship, but when the heavy passion fades, they begin to take their toll.

*   *   *   *

ERNIE'S AND MY COURTSHIP during World War II, which, as I said, was almost entirely by correspondence, gave us scant opportunities to know each other well. My parents had heartily approved of him, first and fore-most because he was a Christian Scientist.

He did not smoke or drink. I admired and respected him. He was well-meaning and a good provider. And although he never abused me physically, he often intimidated me—even though perhaps unintention-ally—and in subtle ways abused me verbally and emotionally.

Over the years, we both began to realize that our attitudes, interests, and tastes diverged. For example, in his view, everything, including home furnishings, must first of all be practical and second of all cheap. Aesthetics was incidental or not important at all. And we realized that our personalities were simply incompatible. We lacked the necessary chemistry required for a solid, lifetime relationship.

During the first ten years of our marriage, I operated a home business—a public stenographic service—to allow Ernie to finish college and obtain a Ph.D. Ten years later, when colleges began offering distance learning pro-grams, I suggested that I might consider pursuing a college degree, believing it would help my self-esteem and job opportunities. But Ernie insisted I did not need a college degree—that it was "just a piece of paper." He failed to express any willingness to do what he could to make this possible for me.

Once he had obtained his Ph.D., he unfortunately fell into the pattern of behaving like a know-it-all. We had a discussion about nuclear power one day. I voiced the intuitive view that the government's plan to subsidize the development of nuclear energy was a big mistake, given all the dangers of radiation exposure and the unresolved problem of nuclear waste disposal. I suggested that in the long term, the same subsidizing funds, if invested in developing alternative energy sources such as solar, wind, and geothermal, would be preferable. Ernie disagreed, asserting that nuclear energy was the best and cheapest answer to the world's energy needs.

It was the way the discussion went that soured me. He made no allowances for my intuitive conclusions and accepted views based exclusively on what he regarded as an analytical, scientific approach with so-called authoritative sources cited chapter and verse. Now with the Fukashima nuclear power disaster and more and more countries abandoning nuclear energy, I feel vindicated that my views should not have been so readily dismissed for a "scientific" assessment.

This scenario repeated itself in discussions about other issues, for example, about genetically modified organisms, GMOs. His intellectual arrogance and dismissal of my views and concerns soon led to my withdrawing and not engaging in discussions with him at all. He didn't like that either. A compulsive talker, he lectured everyone in the family at length on numerous subjects from politics to religion, science, history and men's sexual requirements. He was relentless about telling me and our three daughters what we should do.

I became weary of this, eventually realizing that I was no less intelligent than he was, but that my intelligence ran along different lines.

*   *   *   *

ERNIE AND I REMAINED MARRIED for forty years—1946 to 1986. During the last ten years, I worked out of town during the week, first in Washington, D.C., and then in New York City. My accepting a fascinating job opportunity in a distant city represented a giant step in demonstrating my new self-assertiveness. Predictably, Ernie found himself unprepared to adapt to this arrangement. He couldn't cook. His clothes became moth-eaten. He said it took him eighteen months to adjust to sleeping alone.

Fortunately, Denise and Jeannine stepped up and in their turn managed the household during the workweek while I was away. They did the grocery shopping, cooked, cleaned, and did the laundry.

As for me, I loved the arrangement. A challenging role in a non-profit environmental organization—the National Audubon Society—combined with the privacy of my own tiny apartment in Manhattan thrilled me. I realized I had a great deal of pent-up discomfiture and latent rebellion to deal with. It was not necessarily against people, though I struggled with issues with my mother and Ernie, but also around circumstances. I needed to establish who I was and what I could do on my own. I needed the space and relief from the 24/7 arrangement I had become locked into. And I loved the feeling of economic independence.

Articulating these feelings to Ernie proved painful, but in the end he admitted that all along he had been too dependent on me to take care of him and fulfill all his needs. Eventually he did sometimes help with household chores. In one of my early attempts to be more self-assertive—and with my heart pounding—I had dared to say to him one Saturday morning, "You know, in the twenty-eight years we've been married, you've never once cleaned the toilet. Yet you use it as much, and now even more, than I do."

Some Saturdays later, Ernie emerged from the bathroom, toilet brush in hand. "What gets me," he said, "is that when I do a cleaning job, you never thank me."

"What you're saying is that cleaning is really a woman's job, my job, and that you're doing me a great favor in cleaning up a condition you were at least fifty percent responsible for. Who thanked me all the years I did all the cleaning alone? More often than not, no one even noticed."

He shrank back into the bathroom.

People change and grow, often in different directions. After forty years together, I needed desperately to go my own way. Actually, by that time, neither of us felt comfortable in the marriage.

It took me a month to compose a letter to Ernie expressing my feelings and my reasons for ending the marriage. I didn't want to hurt him. But our relationship had become heavy. The stress relating to our situation was affecting my wellbeing mentally, emotionally, and physically. During a bout with a mild case of shingles, I did a lot of soul searching, taking a hard look at everything about my life, about my past, where I was then, about where my life was headed. This brought me to the conclusion that our marriage no longer served the best interests or personal growth of either of us.

As it turned out, Ernie understood and pursued a no-fault divorce, absent any acrimony. I didn't even have to appear in court. We became better friends than marriage partners. Have I ever regretted marrying Ernie? No. The relationship generated a valuable learning and growing experience for me. And I cherish my daughters.

About eighteen months after our divorce, Ernie married Ruth Newman, a young woman not much older than our eldest daughter. Ruth and I developed a friendly and cordial relationship. There were no hard feelings.

*   *   *   *

FAST FORWARD TO A NEW CENTURY. Ernie and his wife, Ruth, lived in Louisville, Kentucky. Denise and I live in Minnesota. Ernie and I saw each other only rarely and spoke on the phone occasionally. But our daughters visited him from time to time. Around 2007 or so, Ernie's health began to decline. Doctors were unable to diagnose the problem, much less treat it, but they concluded it was neurological. Denise and I suspected that his exposure to heavy metals, especially mercury, over his many years as a chemist, took a severe toll on his body. He also suffered from untreated post traumatic stress disorder (PTSD) stemming from some World War II experiences he would never talk about. Soon he lost the ability to walk and was confined to a wheelchair. In 2009 he became bed-ridden and at the end of the year, he went into a coma. He remained at home with live-in nursing care. In February 2010, Leslie, Denise, and Jeannine all traveled to Louisville to see him. While Leslie and Denise were still there, he passed over early on February 6, about four hours after his eighty-sixth birthday. The final diagnosis: in addition to Parkinson's and PTSD, he had Lewy

Bodies Disease, a neurological condition that cannot be conclusively diagnosed until after a person's demise.

*   *   *   *

AS ONE APPROACHES THE TWILIGHT YEARS, curiosity about the afterlife intensifies. Is there an other side, and if so, what is it like? With Ernie's passing, these questions came to my mind more often, as they had years ago when Bill was killed in the plane crash. Near-death experiences have always been of interest to my daughters and me, though Ernie always pooh-poohed NDEs and any notion of a life beyond the body. He believed there was nothing after death. After his passing, though, my daughters and I came across several books on the subject by Dr. Michael Newton, a hypnotherapist: *Journey of Souls* (July 1994) and *Destiny of Souls* (June 2000).[7] I have read them twice and given copies to a number of friends. Under hypnosis, Dr. Newton's clients describe the experiences they had between lifetimes, and their accounts were remarkably similar. We will, of course, all know what happens one day. For now, the perspectives shared in these books have shifted our awareness considerably.

[7]July 1994 and June 2000, Lewellan Publications, Woodbury, Minnesota.

Chapter 12

Career Stories

I F I HAD IT TO DO OVER AGAIN, I might consider working my way through college to earn a degree in English/creative writing, journalism, or perhaps library science. However, my brother Bill's offer to pay my tuition for business college triggered my decision to pursue secretarial work. After all, I had already mastered touch-typing and Gregg shorthand skills in high school. As it turned out, this career choice served me well, culminating in an executive role by the time I retired in 1995.

All the while, though, I pursued my writing. I read books on creative writing, attended writing conferences and seminars, and studied articles in *The Writer* magazine, to which I have subscribed for fifty years. I educated myself about nonfiction writing without the benefit of a college degree. Years later, I was heartened by a comment made by a reader of my book, *Women Pioneers for the Environment,* who asked me where I had earned my Ph.D. She said the research involved with the book was on a professional academic level.

My work on writing started, as I mentioned, during the first ten years of our marriage. While Ernie was completing his college education, I operated a public stenographic service out of our home, editing and typing doctoral dissertations for graduate students.

Then, one day late in 1967, Ernie came home from his job at DuPont with the news that his boss's boss, Russell W. Peterson, had declared his candidacy for governor of Delaware. Russ had been a research chemist with DuPont for twenty-six years and had supervised the research team that developed Dacron.

"Russ's supporters have created a bi-partisan 'People for Peterson' movement," Ernie said, " and it needs volunteers. Would you be interested in helping?" So, lugging my portable manual typewriter, I showed up for volunteer work a couple mornings a week at "People for Peterson" headquarters housed in the family room of Russ's friends, Sally and Andy Knox.

Several months later, the official Peterson Campaign Committee recruited me to help manage one of its several campaign headquarters. I couldn't have been more ignorant of politics, having no clue what constituted an election district or a convention district. But I learned fast. My role spanned administrative assistant to janitor, including cleaning the toilet and weeding the flower bed. In addition, I operated several office machines and supervised volunteers.

After Russ Peterson won the 1968 election, I settled back into my home management and childrearing role, thinking that was the end of it. But a couple weeks later, I received a phone call from Chris Perry, the governor's executive assistant, in Dover, Delaware. He asked me to help at least part time. This meant a fifty-mile commute from Wilmington, Delaware, to the state capitol. Before long, my position on the governor's staff grew to full time.

* * * *

DURING RUSS PETERSON'S TERM as governor, I undertook a challenging genealogical research project for him on my own time. This was long before ancestry.com.

The morning the airmail letter from Kari Nakling, a Mormon genealogist, arrived, the governor's office teemed with reporters and cameramen setting up for a press conference. I scanned the first sentence of the letter: "Emigration records for the whole country of Sweden have been searched for the year 1881, but the family could not be found." The same old story, I thought—no luck again.

A reporter interrupted me, asking to use my telephone—long before cell phones too.

Glancing back at the letter, I read on: "Birth records have been checked for the entire country (about 2000 parishes). The only one it can possibly be is Johan Anton Petrus Petersson, born 4 January 1868 in Hult parish, Jonkoping County, Smaland."

Letting out a whoop, I sped through the remainder of the letter. I couldn't believe it. Governor Peterson had learned early in 1971 that he would be invited to visit Sweden as an official guest in August that year to participate in the Delaware Day ceremonies in Kalmar (Wilmington's sister city). Ever since then, I had been conducting a search at his request to learn something about the family of his Swedish father. Up until the day the airmail letter from the genealogist in Salt Lake City arrived, I had met with nothing but dead ends in my search.

Rereading the letter, I felt a pang of doubt. Is this really the right family, I wondered? The application for citizenship completed by the governor's father, Johan Anton Peterson, gave his birthday as January 6, not 4, and the year of immigration as 1881, whereas the letter from Salt Lake City said this family emigrated in 1879, two years earlier.

After studying the letter several times, however, I became more convinced that it was probably the correct family, despite the date discrepancies. I was so elated at having obtained the first solid clues about the birthplace of the governor's father and the complete names of the other members of his family that I waited impatiently for the reporters' questions to end that morning so I could tell the governor this exciting personal news. While his office was being cleared of cameras and sound equipment and the furniture restored to order, I told him about the letter. After reading it, he, too was jubilant. For many years Russ had been trying to find out something about his Swedish roots. He felt certain that the family cited in the letter was his. The list of names of his uncles and aunts rang bells in his memory.

That day proved special and gratifying for me—June 24, 1971. That evening a party was held for several Cabinet departments and for the governor's staff. The governor carried in his pocket to the party a copy of the letter and its enclosure—a clerical survey of his father's fam-

ily. During organization of the receiving line, he told the Cabinet secre-
taries standing next to him about his grandfather—Peter Magnus Magnusson. Magnusson? Yes, during the period when this family was born,
patronymic surnames were still being used in Sweden. Thus the sons of
Peter were called Peter's-son. This detail had contributed to making my
detective work exceedingly difficult. After settling in America, Russ Peterson's grandfather assumed the surname all his children bore and was
known as Peter Magnus Peterson.

After months of letter-writing inquiries, and encountering only dead
ends, being on the right track proved especially satisfying. Earlier, I had
been determined—when all responses to my efforts came back negative—
that I would not give up—even if I failed before the governor went to
Sweden in August. It was an exciting challenge.

The information I had to begin my search included only the name and
birthday of the governor's father (that later proved to be off by two days),
the year of immigration (off by two years), plus a few vague recollections
of the governor about possible names of aunts and an uncle—Alma, Frida,
and Gus. It was his impression that they had lived in or near York, Nebraska. He also thought that his grandfather's name might have been Oscar
Peterson. As it turned out, Oscar was an uncle. So my initial probes for information about an Oscar Peterson as head of the family led nowhere.

As a young man, the governor's father, Johan Anton Peterson, left
his Nebraska home and relocated to Portage, Wisconsin, where he married and had a family. When terminally ill and very weak, he completed
an application for citizenship. He had been only eleven years old when
the family immigrated. This probably explains why he remembered
some of the information incorrectly.

The celebrated letter from Salt Lake City came in answer to an in-
quiry I had sent to a genealogical society affiliated with the Mormon
Church. I learned from a pamphlet, "Tracing Your Swedish Ancestry,"
(sent to me by the National Archives in Washington, D.C.) that this society maintained extensive records of Swedish families and that they
would do a search for a small fee.

Earlier I had asked the National Archives to search their passenger ship lists for a New York arrival on the date given on the naturalization record of the Governor's father; but, of course, that date was two years off. National Archives said that passenger ship lists covering the span of years during which this family arrived had never been indexed, and searching them was painstaking and very time-consuming. National Archives, however, gave me a number of leads to other sources of information.

Later in my research, when a closer approximation of arrival date had been determined, National Archives was able to find the passenger list which included Russ's family—the *SS City of Richmond*—which arrived in New York City June 2, 1879.

Documents such as marriage and death certificates that I subsequently obtained confirmed this to be the correct family.

We sent the information I had gathered to officials in Sweden, who assigned someone to search out relatives and locate Russ's father's birthplace in Hult, near Eksjo. During the governor's visit to Sweden in August of 1971, he traveled to the farm where his father had been born and met some distant cousins for the first time.

For months I had been exchanging extensive correspondence with many sources, only a few of which were helpful. Attempts to obtain information from the Census Bureau were particularly frustrating. While none of these early inquiries resulted in success, one of them pointed me to the Genealogical Society in Salt Lake City and to the Emigrant Institute in Vaxjo, Sweden. Kari Nakling, the Mormon genealogist who researched our case, worked on it for eighteen hours and charged me $3.00 an hour.

Following a lead given to me by the Historical Society in Nebraska—the name of a contact in Albion, Nebraska—I located some surviving cousins of the governor. Through this source, I finally obtained missing fragments of information.

Peter Magnus Magnusson and his wife, Agnes Amalia Ekstrom, had nine children, one of whom was Russ Peterson's father, Johan Anton Petrus. Seven of the children were born in Sweden and two in the United States. One Sweden-born child died at sea during the journey to America.

Russ's grandfather had been a farm worker in Sweden. He left Varhult Village to immigrate to the United States. April 18, 1879, sailing from Gothenburg, Sweden, to Liverpool, England, aboard a small vessel called the *Rollo*. In Liverpool the family boarded the *USS Richmond* bound for New York City.

As a birthday gift for Governor Peterson in October 1971, I gave him a scrapbook containing all the genealogical records I had collected on his roots: copies of all my correspondence with the various sources, pedigree charts, naturalization documents, marriage and death certificates, newspaper obituaries, and articles from the Wilmington, Delaware, newspaper about his Swedish heritage and his visit to Sweden, including the royal welcome he received from King Gustaf VI Adolf at the royal palace.

I discovered that Russ's father's youngest sibling, his Aunt Alma, lived in Nebraska. Following some correspondence between them, Russ visited her in a retirement home in Nebraska before she died.

*   *   *   *

Governor Russell W. Peterson with senior staff, Dover, Delaware, 1970.

THE MOST STRESSFUL SITUATION I experienced during Russ's term as governor occurred in 1971 when he asked me to take shorthand notes of his extemporaneous opening remarks at a press conference on the State's budget, then type them up and make copies for the reporters to take as they left the press conference. My stomach churned with the pressure of limited time to complete this assignment.

The outer office where I had to transcribe my notes on a manual typewriter and make the copies buzzed with distracting activities—requests to use the phone and people interrupting me with miscellaneous queries. Deep breathing helped control my shaking under the tension of it all. I finished just as the question and answer session of the press conference ended.

During Russ's tenure as governor of Delaware, two of his many achievements stand out in my memory: he converted an archaic and undemocratic commission form of state government to a streamlined cabinet system, and he led the successful effort against a huge consortium of oil companies led by Shell to pass Delaware's landmark Coastal Zone Management Act protecting the State's coastal area from heavy industry. This Act, the first of its kind in the country, has served as a model for other states.

*   *   *   *

RUSS LOST HIS BID FOR REELECTION in 1972, leaving him with a campaign financial debt. I undertook a fundraising effort, sending letters to his friends and supporters requesting their help. The response exceeded the debt amount, so I returned the excess proportionally to each contributor. Several of them told me they'd never heard of anyone receiving a refund on a contribution.

Much of my work with Russ required researching, writing, and editing skills; e.g., composing draft letters, articles, portions of speeches, brochures, and official documents.

For example, while he was the president of Audubon, he asked me to go over the draft of his keynote speech for the 1986 Leadership Conference on Population, Resources and the Environment to be held in Washington, D.C. I found no mention of the importance of recognizing the roles of women as well as the need to improve their status worldwide before a sustainable balance between resources and population growth could be achieved. "A bad oversight," Russ agreed. "Please write some text about it that I can insert." So I did. A few months later, Russ received a letter from the director of Education at the Wilderness Society expressing appreciation for his comments in that speech on the role of women.

*   *   *   *

NAMING WHAT ONE DOES IN A JOB with an appropriate title is a logical and natural practice—for men. For women, the challenge has been greater to achieve appropriate recognition for the work actually done in a job. Work that was once lumped under the term "secretary" began to be more fully recognized by titles such as executive secretary, administrative assistant, or executive assistant. Yet none of these convey the scope of management skills that most of these jobs require. For example, when Russ became president and CEO of the National Audubon Society in 1979, Audubon did not yet have a Human Resources department. Employees often came to me in the front office for counseling about personnel problems.

Soon after becoming part of the work world full time, I realized management in business and nonprofit organizations paralleled home management in many ways: planning, organizing, setting priorities, managing budgets, maintaining inventories, not to mention volunteer work, which in my case had included being a Girl Scout leader, serving as chairman of an annual book fair at our community school, and serving on the Board of Directors of the local library. Furthermore, home managers often function as a general contractor for home renovation projects: developing a plan, estimating costs, procuring equipment and materials, engaging subcontractors, coordinating the work, and supervising laborers. "Home manager" describes better than "housewife" what many women do. My letter to the editor of *The Christian Science Monitor* on this subject appeared in the August 17, 1984, issue.

In 1981 when I was working with Russ at Audubon, I submitted a memo to him requesting that he consider me a candidate if an appropriate management slot opened up in the organization. To enhance my skills over the years, I had taken several management training courses. And in 1974, I had obtained a Certified Professional Secretary rating (CPS), an internationally recognized standard of excellence for the profession. This involved passing a two-day series of examinations covering six business areas: human relations, business law, economics, accounting and financial analysis, establishing priorities, decision-making, and office procedures (planning, records management, library research, writing). Colleges offered courses to prepare for these examinations, but I studied for the battery of tests independently while working full time. Some of the material I studied stumped Ernie, my Ph.D. husband.

Today, in 2006, while writing this, I wondered whether the International Association of Administrative Professionals still offered a CPS certification examination, given the advancements in technology. So I checked it out on the Internet. The exam is still offered, though modified to fit today's technology. A CPS rating is considered the capstone of the secretarial profession. Holders of the rating (in 2006) numbered 54,000 internationally.

In spite of my appeal, Russ did not assign a departmental management slot to me, asserting that managing the president's office topped any other assignment in the organization. So a couple years later, I submitted another memo to him requesting a change in title—one that would reflect the management role I performed for him and would be recognized in terms that the marketplace could understand, should I need to apply for a job elsewhere in the future. I offered a list of ten possible titles from which he might choose. He did not act on my request immediately. However, in 1984, he named me one of Audubon's vice-presidents and director of the President's Office.

*   *   *   *

I ADMIRED AND RESPECTED RUSS PETERSON. As a passionate environmental activist, he dedicated his life to helping "save the planet." It was my impression that he hoped to make great strides in that direction during his watch at Audubon. Through his leadership and fundraising ability, Audubon's annual budget doubled and the membership grew dramatically. But during budget proposal preparation staff meetings in 1983, I realized that the fundraising goals he had arbitrarily set for senior staff members exceeded what they believed to be realistic. I could sense a chill of alienation and resentment setting in. Suggestions at that time to move Audubon's headquarters to Washington, D.C., created additional uncertainty and stress among staff.

Recently I came across a copy of a long memo I had written to Russ about it. Here's an excerpt:

> The question boils down to what kind of leadership style you wish to use. Yes, you are the boss and can "dictate" how things are going to be, if that's the style you wish to employ. But browbeating people and ram-rodding your view down the throats of your key staff people will not win their cooperation and commitment to your goals. You're dealing with quite a few people who are new in their assignments. Their careers are on the line. They don't want to fail. They need guidance, nurturing, teaching, encouragement, friendly persuasion—and need to feel that they are involved in the decisions being made—not having decisions handed to them—decisions they are not yet convinced are sound.

> During the difficult year ahead, there are going to be many dislocations, disruptions, and reorganization. It is no time to compound our problems by fostering resentment, discouragement, lack of support for your decisions by using a management style that is alienating your staff.

With Russ Peterson and Margaret Mead, New Directions, Washington, D.C., 1977.

Wow! Today I wonder how I ever found the nerve to tell off my boss so frankly. But Russ eased up on the budget goals. And the move of Audubon headquarters to Washington never took place.

I worked intermittently with Russ for thirteen years: during his term as Delaware's governor, when he was CEO of a fledgling nonprofit venture called New Directions, in D.C., when he served as director of the Office of Technology Assessment of the U.S. Congress in Washington, D.C., and during his six years as president and CEO of the National Audubon Society in New York City. While my main home base remained in Wilmington, Delaware, where I spent weekends, I also maintained an apartment in Washington while I worked there. And I kept an apartment in Manhattan during the years I worked for Audubon.

Russ told me that the way I had categorized and organized his huge collection of documents over the years had played a role in the Library of Congress wanting him to donate his papers to the Library on his retirement. They approached him about it four times before he finally gave them his collection in 2004.

Although Russ originally registered as a Republican, his views more accurately aligned with those of Democrats. He endorsed Jimmy Carter for president in 1980 and became a Democrat himself in 1986. While president of the National Audubon Society, Russ fought vigorously President Ronald Reagan's efforts to weaken the enforcement of environmental regulations. He retorted to Reagan's comment that conservationists would never be happy until the White House became a bird's nest by remarking that the White House was already a "cuckoo's nest."

Russ retired from Audubon in 1986, but I remained with Audubon in my same role for ten more years, working with his successor, Peter Berle.

After retiring from Audubon, Russ wrote a couple books and received numerous honors: a Lifetime Achievement Award from his alma mater, the University of Wisconsin Alumni Association, and an award from the League of Women Voters. He received fifteen honorary doctorates, including one from the University of Delaware. As well, he became a luminary in Delaware and became known as one of Delaware's environmental giants. An urban Wildlife Refuge in Wilmington bears his name and features a statue of him. Russ continued an active life working for environmental causes until he was ninety-four. He passed on very quickly a few hours after suffering a stroke on February 21, 2011.

* * * *

BETWEEN STINTS WORKING with Russ Peterson I held positions with a couple corporations. For two years, from 1974 to 1976, I worked for DuPont in Wilmington, Delaware. During that time, Russ was Chairman of the President's Council on Environmental Quality (CEQ) in Washington, D.C.

One day while sitting across the desk from my DuPont boss, Harlan Wendall, assistant director of DuPont's Public Affairs Department, I listened as he ticked off compliments about my work. Then he paused, and after reflecting for a moment, blurted out, "But your ambition is showing." The way he said it communicated that my demonstration of initiative was a negative quality in his view. I wondered if he would have viewed a male employee who showed initiative in a different light.

Ah—the despised Performance Evaluation—a new experience for me, even though by then I had been in the work world full time for six years

My role at DuPont—on special assignment to the director and assistant director of the Public Affairs Department—involved, among other things, my functioning as research and editorial assistant, reviewing and abstracting articles, preparing quick-reference briefing books for top corporate executives, and writing sections of the departmental office manual. I also reorganized the records management system of my bosses. Sometimes I substituted as an executive secretary to DuPont corporate executives, including the president and chairman of the Board, Irving Shapiro at that time.

After the performance evaluation session with my boss, I speculated about what I might have done to warrant his comment about my "ambition showing." At the time, 1975, the U.S. Congress was preparing to pass the Toxic Substances Control Act (TSCA). The Manufacturing Chemists Association had asked DuPont's Public Affairs Department to produce a brochure setting forth the chemical industry's position on the issue. I had organized the textual material at hand on the subject and designed a brochure. The final document closely resembled what I had put together.

Had I stepped on the toes of someone in the department, I wondered, who then complained about me to my boss? Who knows?

As an environmentalist, the substance of this project did not reflect my own viewpoint on the issue, so undertaking it posed an ethical conflict. But I did it anyway. The Toxic Substances Control Act of 1976 was badly flawed, grandfathering over 62,000 chemicals without any testing or proof of safety. And under that law, the Environmental Protection Agency had no authority to ban even the most dangerous substances, such as asbestos, formaldehyde, and lead. In 2012, Dr. Richard Denison, a chemical scientist with the Environmental Defense Fund, stated that "Every American is contaminated with toxic chemicals because of the failure of TSCA. For too long people have been involuntary guinea pigs for chemical testing."[8] The Safe Chemicals Act that includes a few essential reforms now creeps along through Congress.

After working two years at DuPont, I felt fed up with the huge chemical corporation, so I left. At the time I resigned, I had just been promoted to a staff assistant position, considered a step up in the corporate hierarchy.

* * * *

BETWEEN 1976 AND 1979 I WORKED with Russ at the Office of Technology Assessment in Washington, D.C, weekdays, returning as usual by Amtrak's Metroliner train to my primary home in Wilmington, Delaware, on weekends. For the most part, I enjoyed being in Washington, D.C., and having the opportunity to visit the Congressional buildings, the museums, the Library of Congress, and the monuments.

I'll always remember one morning as I walked to the OTA office from the subway station, I saw a digital display on a bank building that read "7/7/77, 77 degrees."

My memory of those few in years in D.C. is marred by two attempted criminal attacks. One occurred as I rode an escalator up to street level from the Eastern Market subway station. A man tried to grab my handbag. I hung on, however, and he didn't get away with it.

The second incident terrified me.

It happened in broad daylight around 8:00 p.m. on a June evening in 1978. My apartment building was located across the street from the then-location of the Russian embassy and was considered a safe neighborhood. As I turned away from the asphalt-paved alley and headed into the rear entrance of my apartment building on Sixteenth Street, I heard the rapid pounding footfalls of someone close behind me. A strong arm swung me around, slamming me hard against the side-wall of the entrance way, making me drop a rolled up throw rug I had fetched from the cleaners on my way home from work.

---

[8] *Solutions*, Environmental Defense Fund periodical, Fall 2012 issue, p. 11.

As I had been walking along the alley, I had noticed a young boy ahead of me going in the same direction. He wore a white polo shirt, a baseball cap, blue shorts, and tennis shoes. He looked clean and non-threatening. But I noticed that as he walked along ahead of me, at one point he looked back and saw me. When I turned into the apartment back entrance-way, he raced back, seizing me just as I was about to open the apartment building door.

Exposing himself, he attempted to rape me. He was unarmed. While I struggled with him, I screamed for help. At this point in my life, I had not yet learned basic self-defense techniques women can use under these circumstances, such as a swift knee in the attacker's crotch or poking my fingers in his eyes. But my screams drew attention. He fled as help approached. Someone called the police. Shaking, I collapsed onto the sleep sofa in my studio apartment. A policeman arrived to obtain a description of the boy. My only fragment of evidence was a button I discovered clutched in my hand. I must have torn it off his polo shirt during the struggle. As far as I know, the attacker was never apprehended. From that day on, I used only the front street entrance to my apartment.

By contrast, for sixteen years—from 1979 to 1995—I worked in New York City during Mayor Ed Koch's administration. Only *once*, during my last few months there, was I victimized by a crime. I write about this incident in a later chapter about vacation stories.

*   *   *   *

DURING THE FINAL TEN YEARS of my work-world career, I continued in my position at the National Audubon Society, working with Peter A.A. Berle, who succeeded Russ Peterson as president and CEO in 1986. Peter, an environmental attorney, had served three terms in the New York State Assembly and was the former commissioner of Environmental Conservation for the State of New York.

Audubon then occupied several floors of rental space in a building on the corner of Fifty-ninth Street and Second Avenue. Obtaining its own

With Govenor Russell W. Peterson (left) and Peter A.A. Berle.

building had been a primary goal of the organization for some time. Under Peter Berle's leadership, Audubon purchased a vacant historic building at 700 Broadway. Following green construction values, such as using recycled materials, the building underwent gutting and total renovation. It became a showcase for green architecture. During an Audubon whale-watching trip to Baja California in 1994, I gave an on-board talk about our new headquarters, accompanied by slide photos I had taken.

Fairly early in Peter Berle's ten years as president and CEO of Audubon, a senior person at a staff meeting suggested that a new, more modern, logo might be a good idea to reenergize the organization. She recommended we engage a New York City designer of high repute (as well as a high fee, I might add).

To replace Audubon's famous traditional flying egret logo, the designer came up with a wavy blue flag with Audubon's name across it. I thought it was ugly and stupid, but I held back from voicing my views, believing my humble opinion would weigh nothing against work done by a professional designer.

In an effort to promote the new logo's acceptance throughout the organization, T-shirts, letterhead, and even coffee mugs soon appeared featuring the design. A T-shirt displaying the proposed logo even appeared in my in-box.

Audubon's legendary flying egret logo (top), and the ill-fated proposal (bottom).

But when the new logo reached our field offices and local chapter leaders, all hell broke loose. A major rebellion erupted. The idea of abandoning the historic and legendary flying egret logo stirred deep emotions among the grassroots members. Furthermore, they hadn't even been consulted about it—a major faux pas for a nonprofit that depends on its membership.

It quickly became obvious that the new logo would never be accepted, much less used, by the local chapters. Peter acknowledged our mistake, and we reinstated the flying egret logo, only slightly modified from the original design.

I still have my T-shirt displaying the defunct logo. I've never worn it, but who knows, it may become a collector's item.

My years with Audubon included a few bumps. I had run-ins with an over-aggressive and bossy woman Peter Berle had hired to be senior vice-president for Development. She ran roughshod over everyone, butting into every department's business and telling people what to do. At one point, she gave me an uncalled for dressing-down on the telephone. As much as I felt like doing something physical in response, I settled on sending her a memo telling her off. I also vented my spleen about her in a couple memos to Peter.

Another incident hit me hard. The day before the formal public showcase opening celebration of Audubon's new green headquarters at 700 Broadway in New York early in 1994, I undertook a major project—unpacking, cleaning arranging and hanging John James Audubon's orig-

Avian artwork of John James Audubon and busts of him and wife, Lucy, in the conference room of National Audubon Society's headquarters, a renovated historic building in New York City.

inal avian artwork in the conference room, reception area, and the president's suite, plus cleaning and placing busts of Audubon and his wife, Lucy. Curators and staff in museums are paid well to design and arrange exhibits. In fact, Audubon's ornithologist staff member, Susan Drennan, had been assigned this task. But when she failed to make it happen, I used my initiative to do it and finished the job just hours before the opening. At the gathering to mark the opening the next day, Senior Vice-President Jim Cunningham, who had always been a good friend, publicly gave all the credit for this to Susan Drennan. She had done nothing to help me. I thought she might pipe up at that point, but she didn't.

I felt invisible, demoralized, and unappreciated, so much so that I could not bring myself to attend Peter's party that evening. He called me after the party to find out why I had not come. I told him.

The next morning at the Audubon Board meeting, Peter tried to fix it up, but as far as I was concerned, he only made it sound as though I was Audubon's scrub-woman. I wrote a note to Jim Cunningham spilling my anger. He apologized profusely.

* * * *

View in Central Park, Manhattan, 5:30 a.m., May 1995 Audubon Birdathon.

Ornithologist Kevin Kauffman, center, during an Audubon Birdathon, 1990.

With Audubon President Peter Berle, Jamaica Bay, Queens, 1995 Audubon Birdathon.

With President Jimmy Carter and Rosalynn in Fort Myers, Florida, November 1994.

EACH MAY, AUDUBON'S ANNUAL fundraising Birdathon offered a pleasant daylong outing away from the office. Peter Berle and I, accompanied by a couple Audubon ornithologists and several senior staff members, sought out as many different bird species as possible in the greater New York Metropolitan area. Congregating at 5:04 a.m. in the parking lot in Central Park, we took off for our first foray of the day down the Park's "Ramble." Central Park at dawn is mystical and enchanting. An enlarged and framed photograph of a Central Park early morning scene that I shot during our Birdathon in May 1995 hangs in my home office here in St. Paul.

During our Birdathons in the 1990s, we peered through our binoculars to check out the progress of "Pale Male," a red-tailed hawk that gained fame when he began nesting on a precarious ledge on the eighth floor of an historic and swanky high-rise on Fifth Avenue at Seventy-fourth Street overlooking Central Park. After several years of trying, he and a mate finally fledged chicks, causing even non-birding New Yorkers to go atwitter. As I write this more than a decade later, I have learned that Pale Male has survived three mates, has taken a fourth and all told has fledged twenty-four chicks over the years from his Fifth Avenue aerie.

The mid-day venue of our annual Birdathon outing was usually Jamaica Bay with its plethora of shorebirds.

A peak experience of my years with Audubon occurred when former President Jimmy Carter attended our Annual Dinner in November 1994 to receive the prestigious Audubon Medal. The event took place in Fort Myers, Florida, and included an afternoon birding expedition that the Carters had requested. In preparation for these events, I worked closely for weeks with the Secret Service personnel assigned to accompany the Carters everywhere they went. Later, in 1998, I corresponded with President Carter, sending him, at his request, some resources on birding.

On returning from the birding field trip with the Carters, several Audubon folks stopped me on the street to congratulate me, but I had no idea what for. It turned out that, in my absence, I had won a raffle drawing worth an all-expenses-paid trip for two to New Brunswick, the eastern-most province of Canada.

Peter planned to leave Audubon in August 1995 and I decided (then at age seventy-one) to retire also. After twenty-seven years in the work world, my gross annual salary had climbed to over $87,000.

One of Audubon's Birdathons.

Another Audubon Birdathon.

In 1996, after both Peter Berle and I had retired from Audubon, Peter and his wife, Lila, invited me one weekend to a cider-making party at their Sky Farm in the Berkshires, near Stockbridge, Massachusetts. I took a train from Wilmington, Delaware, to Albany, New York, where Peter met me and drove me to the farm. We spent part of Saturday cleaning the antique cider press that had gathered dust in the barn.

After other guests arrived, we all began picking apples in the orchard that covered a rather steep hillside. Walking down the hill, I stepped on a slippery rotten apple, skidded, and fell down with my left foot twisted under me. I hobbled back up the hill to the barn and found an up-turned bucket to sit on for the remainder of the day watching the other guests make cider.

Once the guests had departed, Peter decided it would be wise to take me to a local emergency room. He carried me to his pick-up truck and took me there. I had indeed fractured my left ankle. The medics fitted me with a temporary splint and crutches, advising me to see an orthopedic physician immediately on arriving back in Wilmington.

Peter realized how difficult it would be for me on crutches to travel home by train. So he arranged for a private car and driver to take me all the way to Wilmington from Stockbridge the following day—a 250-mile trip. We met the car and driver in front of the Red Lion Inn on Main Street in Stockbridge. Peter helped load me, my crutches, and my suitcase into the car, leaned in to give me a peck on the cheek, and instructed the driver to escort me and my luggage all the way up to my third floor Rodney Court apartment in Wilmington. Hiring this private car must have cost Peter dearly.

In August 2007 I received a telephone call from Graham Cox, a former Audubon colleague.

"Peter asked me to call you," he said, "he's been badly injured in a serious accident."

"Was he driving?"

"No, it was not an auto accident. He and a hired man were taking down an old shed on the Berle farm near Stockbridge. The roof collapsed on Peter, crushing him. The hired man lifted the roof off Peter with a tractor. Peter is in intensive care at the Berkshire Medical Center in Pittsfield, Massachusetts. He has a broken back and severe internal injuries. He's already had three operations, one of which lasted over nine hours. The doctors say if he survives, he'll need to wear a back brace for at least four months."

Peter Berle was strong and athletic, a competitive runner, skier, swimmer, hiker, mountain climber. I had high hopes his body would heal. But he was diabetic—a complicating factor.

Immediately I undertook writing regular notes of encouragement and support to him and his wife, Lila.

About a week later I called the hospital to see how he was doing, expecting to speak either with Lila or his daughter, Mary, who were sitting with him in shifts. But neither one was in his room. A nurse answered.

"Who's calling?" she asked.

"It's Mary Joy."

Peter asked for the phone.

"It's so good to hear your voice," he said.

"Yours, too" I replied. Then he proceeded to describe the shed accident.

Soon after that, Peter had to be put on a respirator and was unable to talk. So I was glad I had called when I did.

Peter was in and out of intensive care, had many ups and downs and additional surgeries for infection and for fluid in his lungs. At several points, the medical team said he came close to dying. But Peter seemed to be making slow but steady improvement. Graham Cox and other former Audubon colleagues who were able to visit Peter or talk with Lila by telephone, kept me and other friends and associates up to date on his condition with almost daily e-mails.

The medical team took him off the respirator and he began having daily physical therapy sessions. We all thought he had turned a corner and would pull through.

Then, on November 1st after more than two months of tenacious struggling to heal his body, Peter returned to his bed after a physical therapy session, smiled at his wife, Lila, and daughter, Mary, then closed his eyes. He never opened them again. He was sixty-nine years old. It feels like a tragedy that never should have happened.

I recall the ten years I worked as Peter's sidekick at Audubon as the most exciting and enjoyable time of my twenty-seven-year working career. My time working with him was never dull, and he had a remarkable spirit about him.

* * * *

IN MAY 1995, I RECEIVED a telephone call from an editor at Northeastern University Press in Boston, inquiring about my interest in writing a book. I almost fell off my chair in disbelief. This is an unheard of experience for an unknown writer. Although I had had numerous articles published, I had never undertaken writing a book.

Here's how it came about. Over the years as items crossed my desk, I had saved information about women environmental activists worldwide. During an Audubon gathering out West one year, I told an elderly woman activist—Hazel Wolf—about some of these women. She asked me to share copies of my collection. Later, she requested my permission to use the material I had sent her in speeches she gave to school children. The editor at Northeastern University Press had seen a copy of one of Hazel's speeches in an Earth Island Institute newsletter. He called her about writing a book.

"You have the right subject, but the wrong author," she told him. "I didn't collect any of this research and am not a writer." She referred him to me. Actually *she* had been urging me for a number of years to write such a book. But my demanding job left me no time to do it. But with my forthcoming retirement plans, researching and writing a book became feasible.

Following my departure from Audubon in August of 1995, I took a brief vacation with a friend, using my raffle-winning ticket for the trip to New Brunswick.

For the next three years I became a recluse, researching and writing *Women Pioneers for the Environment*. The book tells the stories of forty-two women from thirteen countries around the world who stepped out of traditional roles to become passionate environmental activists on various issues. The book came out in hardback in 1998 and in paperback in 2000. Reviews were excellent, including a glowing blurb by Ralph Nader.

Preparing the book's index became the most difficult part of writing the book. The publisher said I would have to pay for a professional indexer if I didn't want to undertake the task myself. No way. So, after studying the *Chicago Manual of Style* section on indexing, I plunged in. Gratification came when my editor commented that she had seen indexes less well done than mine by professional indexers.

After Peter Berle left Audubon, he launched an environmental program for public radio. He interviewed me about my book for one of his segments.

Women Pioneers for the Environment is still listed (as of 2014) on Amazon's website. In 2002 Northeastern University Press merged with the University Press of New England, a consortium of six New England academic presses. Their fall 2006 catalog included my book in their back-list of books on women's studies.

In 2002, an editor at Harvard University Press saw the piece in my book about Katharine Ordway. The editor assigned me to write a 1000-word essay about Ordway for their newest supplement to Harvard University Press's *Notable American Women* series, a library reference book. The supplement, covering the years 1975 to 2000, came out in 2005.

Today in the twenty-first century, my career still rolls along. In 2002, Denise and I co-founded a small nonprofit publishing venture called Living Justice Press focusing on restorative justice. We operate the business out of the home we share in St. Paul. Denise is the executive director. As such she handles a great many administrative tasks—editing manuscripts, creating indexes, managing arrangements for cover designs, printing and e-book conversions, as well as preparing invoices and filling orders. I serve as secretary/treasurer, processing incoming book sales money for deposit, paying bills, managing records, doing marketing research, proof reading, and helping prepare for Board meetings. By 2013, we have produced eleven titles, two of which received Silver Medals (second prize) in the Independent Publishers Book Awards program. Our first title, *Peacemaking Circles: From Crime to Community* is in its fourth print run!

Our efforts to obtain foundation grants for our nonprofit venture met with only minimal success. So in an effort to gain income from increased book sales, I engaged in extensive Internet research.

On the fringes of my work for Living Justice Press, I have been writing this autobiography.

Recently the Minnesota Historical Society launched a four-year project to create a searchable computer Internet database of stories by Minnesotans who lived through the Great Depression, through World War II and through the so-called "Boom" decade of the 1950s. Stories could be no longer than 8000 characters. But contributors could submit multiple stories. I wrote sixteen pieces. The project editor, Linda Cameron at the Minnesota Historical Society, posted all of them. The Historical Society named the database "Share Your Story—the Greatest Generation."

Chapter 13

Children

ERNIE WAS NOT ENTHUSIASTIC about having children, and his attitude stemmed from his teen-age exposure to the soiled diaper stench of his Uncle Henry's babies. But he went along with my wish to have children. I realized he would not help much with infant care. In fact, the one time he changed a soiled diaper, he retched so badly I never asked him to change a diaper again.

Although at that time I knew nothing about the symptoms of Asperger's Syndrome, in hindsight—and after observing many aspects of Ernie's behavior over the years—I have come to believe he had Asperger's. Asperger people are just wired differently, and the patterns associated with Asperger's span a spectrum. Heightened sensory sensitivity is one of the characteristics, as is compulsive talking.

We raised three daughters, the first two born while Ernie was still in graduate school. Leslie Jeanne Breton was born July 21, 1949, in Fort Leonard Wood, Missouri; Denise Christine Breton was born November 1, 1953, in Gainesville, Florida; and Jeannine Breton, was born April 15, 1961, in Wilmington, Delaware.

All three girls plowed their way through traumatizing episodes in their adult lives. Today I reflect on what I might have done differently as a parent to prevent these heart-wrenching experiences. Certainly, my working away from home during the week was a major factor. Women continue to struggle to balance the demands of work and careers with the demands of motherhood, especially since society continues to place far lower expectations on men as fathers to shoulder their share of the

119

responsibilities. Had Ernie's and my relationship been stronger and had he been more committed to fathering, the experience for us as a family and for our children would have been different. He tried to be a good father and was in many ways, but his head was in his work, as was mine.

As a result, we were not there for our daughters many times during critical growing up and teen years, especially for our youngest, Jeannine. Now it is more expected that children come home to an empty house until one or both of their parents arrive home from work. I began working part time for Russ's campaign for governor when Jeannine was six and starting school, and I began working in Washington during the week when she was fifteen. More than once, Ernie's work took him away on business trips that left Jeannine alone in the house for extended periods of time, the other daughters having grown up and left. Jeannine matured at an early age, and the family had good relations with a neighbor. Still, she was not eighteen, and no matter how mature young people behave, they still need their parents. Looking back, I cannot fathom why neither of us arranged for someone to be there. This was terribly wrong, and it pains me to think of it.

Jeannine almost died once as a result. That was in 1978. During the week, I was in Washington, D.C., working at the Office of Technology Assessment for U.S. Congress. Ernie and Jeannine were the only ones living in Wilmington. Our other two daughters had left home. Jeannine was feeling sick, and she told her father so as he was leaving for a business trip. He told her he hoped she felt better and left for the airport. One of Jeannine's Tatnall School classmates saved her life. When she described her symptoms to him over the phone, he sped over, carried her out to the car, and rushed her to the Emergency Room. She had developed a severe infection and would not have survived without medical and even hospital care.

The stakes are ultimate for children when parents have to balance childrearing and career. As many job applicants discover, the better and higher paying jobs usually require business trips or long-distance working arrangements. Now with the Internet, parents have many more options for being home with the children and maintaining a good job. Our family got caught in a transition, as women started moving out into the work world but found little support from their husbands, employers, or society. I am grateful beyond words every day that my choices and Ernie's did not result in Jeannine's death, and I will be forever grateful to the classmate who saved her. We came so close.

Jeannine has grown up to become a self-reliant individual, which she had to become. She has excelled in her work life and career, and she is a most devoted parent to two children. I admire her immensely. Other children might not have been able to do this.

One thing for sure, we have a long way to go as a society in meeting the needs of working parents, their children, and their lives together as families. Some working parents now put their children in daycare routinely, sometimes as early as a few weeks or months after birth. I was a full-time Mom for Jeannine for six years and for my older daughters longer. Society's expectations and values around childrearing have changed. Unlike the extended family and community models of many Indigenous and traditional societies, the nuclear family model puts enormous demands on the parents to provide everything for their children on every level. Children inevitably pay the price. As I said, all three of our daughters have been through rough times. I leave it to them to tell about their experiences should they ever decide to do so.

However, I feel free to relate a few stories about them.

* * * *

LESLIE LOVED BOOKS AND EXHIBITED a high level of intelligence, scoring 140 on an IQ test. But when she entered first grade in 1955, her teacher, fresh out of teachers' college, used the then-trendy look-say/Dick-and-Jane system of teaching children to read. It involved rote memorization of whole words to teach reading. According to this approach, phonics should be taught only as a last resort.

The look-and-say system did not work for Leslie. Fortunately I discovered a book by Rudolph Flesch entitled *Why Johnny Can't Read and What You Can Do about It.*[9]

[9]Harper and Rowe, New York, New York, 1955.

This blockbuster book remained on the best-seller list for thirty weeks and triggered a raging controversy among educators, researchers and parents that continues even today. The "Look and Say" method spread to Britain in the 1950s, but studies have shown that the method has been a disaster for literacy levels in both England and the United States. Some researchers believe that it actually dumbs down students and possibly exacerbates dyslexia and attention deficit disorder.[10]

Educators were abandoning the teaching of phonics, causing many youngsters to fail to learn to read. Today many parents, researchers, and even teachers blame the Dick & Jane look/say system for many Americans' poor reading skills. Dr. Seuss (Theodor Geisel) regretted the association of his books, like *The Cat in the Hat*, with the "look-say" movement. He said, "I think killing phonics was one of the greatest causes of illiteracy in the country."[11] Author-educator Samuel L. Blumenfeld suggested that parents teach their children to read phonetically before giving them the Dr. Seuss books.

I obtained a teachers' manual and phonic primer published by Northwestern University Press (recommended by Flesch) and taught Leslie to read. The phonics method teaches the alphabet and the sound each letter makes. The beauty of the phonic system is that once children learn to recognize letters and the sounds they make, even many large words can be deciphered—or sounded out. Leslie quickly caught on and became an avid reader and writer. Early on, she composed a series of stories about a squirrel she called Peppi.

Rudolph Flesch wrote a second book twenty-five years after the first—*Why Johnny STILL Can't Read.*[12] It, too, became a best seller. But the education establishment not only ignored his work but also ridiculed him. Educators had to know that the look-say system didn't work, but they kept it going anyway.

---

[10]Sam L. Blumfeld, *New Illiterates and How to Keep Your Child from Becoming One*, Paradigm Co., 1988; see also Nick Gibb, *Johnny Can Read if Only He's Given a Chance*, The Telegraph Media Group Lilmited, September 26, 2012.
[11]Arizona magazine, June 1981.
[12]Harpercollins, New York, New York, May 25, 1983.

*   *   *   *

FOUR YEARS AFTER LESLIE'S BIRTH, Denise came along in 1953 while Ernie worked for his Ph.D. at the University of Florida. One hot summer day in Gainesville, Florida, as I worked on a doctoral dissertation for a graduate student, Leslie rushed in, sweat pouring down her face.

Denise's first birthday, in a wagon with Leslie, November 1954.

"Denise ran away."

Denise, barefoot, clad only in a diaper and scarcely eighteen months old, had ventured out on her own down the street and across intersections.

"I couldn't stop her," Leslie panted. "She kept pushing me away." Fearing the worst, I tore out of the house and sprinted in the direction she had been heading, Leslie trotting behind me. I suspected where she wanted to go.

A new Kroger supermarket in Gainesville a few blocks away from our house had festooned their store with red, white and blue balloons for their opening celebration. We had shopped there several days earlier. Sure enough, I soon caught up with Denise who was toddling along at a rapid clip toward the store. As I scooped her up, she pointed down the street, jabbering about balloons. So we strolled on to satisfy Denise's yen to admire the balloons again.

One morning when Denise was about two years old, my British friend, Phil Calkins, and I were enjoying our tea and scones at the kitchen table when I noticed an unusual silence in the house. Uh-oh, time to check on what the kids are up to. Leslie had her nose buried in a book in her room. Farther down the hall, I discovered Denise sitting on the floor in my bedroom in front of the dressing table I had cobbled together with orange crates and a fabric skirt. Holding a jar of face cream, she had slathered the cream not only on her face but also on her bare belly.

*   *   *   *

AFTER ERNIE OBTAINED HIS PH.D. at the University of Florida, we relocated to Chester County in southeastern Pennsylvania, just over the border from Delaware. Ernie had accepted a position as research chemist at the DuPont Experimental Station in Wilmington.

By this time, Denise was five years old. In another chapter I wrote about our Pennsylvania experience. But during our two years living in that mushroom farming community, Denise and I undertook a special creative project together.

The December 1956 issue of *Better Homes and Gardens* magazine featured instructions for crafting a Nativity crèche from mostly natural materials. So one day in late autumn, Denise and I, toting a paper sack, set out to tramp the nearby fields in search of what we needed—corn stalks, corn husks, wheat straws, and acorns. Several necessary items required a visit to a craft store: raffia, yarn, gold paint, fabric dye, pipe cleaners, a tiny baby doll, and several plastic lambs.

A wire coat hanger, concealed by corn stalks, provided the frame for the stable. Using raffia, we lashed wheat straws together to form the walls and roof. While we worked on the manger, corn husks soaked for several days in four one-quart Ball canning jars filled with blue, green, red, and yellow fabric dye.

The Ntivity crèche that Denise and I created, in 1959.

Cones, cut and formed from manila file folders, became the figures' bodies, with pipe cleaners for arms and acorns for heads. We draped the dyed corn husks as robes around the figures. Denise gilded the caps of the acorn crowns on the Three Kings.

Until recently, every holiday season since we created the Nativity creche in 1958, we have displayed it under our Christmas tree. However, it has become extremely fragile and is beginning to fall apart. It now rests in its special box in our basement. I can't bring myself to dispose of it yet.

*   *   *   *

DENISE'S FIRST GRADE TEACHER terrorized the students in an effort to maintain her performance record for reading achievement. Denise went off to school each morning with fear and dread in her heart. I didn't wait for Denise to have difficulty learning to read under this tyrant. From the get-go, I taught her the phonic system at home.

The study of Greek history and culture in Denise's high school social studies class at Friends School required each student to undertake a special relevant project. Denise chose to prepare and serve to her classmates a meal of Greek cuisine:

Dolmades – stuffed grape leaves (rice, onions, seasonings)

Spanikopita – spinach pie with phyllo, also called filo, crust

Oktapodi – octopus in red wine sauce

Tsoureki – a sweet bread

Baklava pastry – layers of phyllo dough filled with butter, chopped nuts, and honey

Mr. Smith, the social studies teacher, found the scene highly amusing. He enjoyed the challenge of persuading teenage kids to try some strange new foods. Wanting to be good sports, the students scrutinized the buffet selections and tried most of them. The notion of eating octopus, however, failed to have much appeal. One student, a wrestler, in fact, could not keep it down later during wrestling practice. Of course, the baklava dessert was a hit.

Early on, Denise often engaged me in conversations about spirituality, asking me questions I found difficult or impossible to answer. When she became a teenager, she also pushed her Christian Science Sunday School teachers with questions. It was inevitable that she would go her own way on the big questions of life. Denise majored in philosophy and world religions. She is a published author and is now working on her fifth book.

*   *   *   *

I LAY FLAT ON MY BACK in the hospital delivery room with my legs still strapped in stirrups and my wrists clamped to the table. The male obstetrician and nurse had disappeared, leaving me alone and unable to reach my nine-pound newborn, Jeannine, lying in an incubator ten feet away from me (unable even to ring for help if need be). This barbaric, disrespectful, and humiliating treatment of birthing still held sway in 1961. If I had it to do over again, I would engage a midwife for a home delivery.

Family photo, left to right: Denise, Jeannine, Ernie, me, and Leslie, 1964.

In the meantime, Ernie, Leslie, and Denise sat in the hospital waiting room, wondering why it was taking so long to hear news of me. They knew how close I had come to giving birth in the car on the way to the hospital in Wilmington, Delaware. Finally, after what I judged to be more than half an hour, a nurse reappeared, unstrapped me, took me to my room, and whisked Jeannine off to the nursery.

Having had male obstetricians for Leslie and Denise, I

My daughter Leslie's son, Eric.

My youngest daughter, Jeannine, and her son, David, 1995.

My grandson, David, Jeannine's son, in 2013.

had chosen a woman for this third pregnancy. But Jeannine arrived a week later than her due date. Unbeknownst to me, my woman OB had taken off to a medical conference in Miami, Florida. Her stand-in, a man I first glimpsed in the delivery room, would certainly never have been my choice.

As with Leslie and Denise, I taught Jeannine phonics from the start. She attended first and second grade in the Avondale elementary school in Chester County, Pennsylvania. After we moved across the border into Delaware, we enrolled her in Tatnall, a private school, where she graduated in 1979.

In 1969, when Jeannine was eight years old, I joined the work world full time. Denise, then fifteen or sixteen, assumed many of the home management responsibilities, including cooking meals and mothering Jeannine.

Jeannine loves animals. When she was six, she had a pet flying squirrel that had found its way into our Carriage House. She called the squir-

My granddaughter, Johanna (Josie), Jeannine's daughter, 2013.

Jeannine's daughter, Johanna (Josie), and me, 2001.

rel "Squeaky." This tiny nocturnal creature often snoozed in Jeannine's pocket during the day.

Her animals while growing up also included a miniature poodle, a cat, and a parakeet. As an adult, she has included in her adult household a fish aquarium, a number of cats, a parrot, some parakeets, and several border collie dogs, not to mention turtles and toads. When she had children, she decided to homeschool them for a time. To teach them about the creatures who live in the ponds around their home, she developed a small aquarium that held leeches, pond plants, snails, and other life on the kitchen table. Her children spent hours watching them.

Jeannine has also had a longtime interest in gardening, learning a great deal about it from conversations with experienced gardeners—her Great Uncle Fremont and my mother. As a teenager, she put into practice what she learned by creating a vegetable patch near our Carriage House patio.

Beginning in 1979, I worked in Manhattan weekdays. Sometimes one of the girls came to New York for a weekend with me. One weekend I took Jeannine to see *Cats* at the Wintergarden Theatre on Broadway. We also enjoyed the Circle tour boat ride around Manhattan Island; we visited the Trump Tower, Rockefeller Center, and Rizzoli's famous bookstore. We went to see Jean Stapleton on stage in *Arsenic and Old Lace* and visited the South Street Seaport in Greenwich Village, where we watched Stacy Keach filming a new TV *Mike Hammer* episode on the street.

Of the plethora of restaurants in Manhattan, two stand out in my memory as offering memorable experiences. Who could ever forget eating and celebrating at the Russian Tea Room next to Carnegie Hall on Fifty-seventh Street? With its glorious samovar-studded, painting-filled décor of red and gold, it resembled a palace. Whenever one of my daughters visited New York City during the 1980s, I splurged and treated her to a splendid meal there: often chicken Kiev, borscht, and chocolate mousse.

And during another weekend, Jeannine and I, after browsing the special amber exhibit at the Metropolitan Museum of Art, delighted in savoring French specialties, such as ratatouille at my other favorite restaurant—the Brasserie.

Both restaurants went out of business in the early 2000s. I cried when I read an article in the *New York Times* in 2002 about the closing of the Russian Tea Room.

Ultimately both Leslie and Denise graduated from Wilmington Friends School, and Jeannine finished high school at Tatnall School. Leslie studied nursing at the University of Delaware. Denise majored in philosophy and world religions for her degree; and Jeannine chose chemistry as her field.

* * * *

I HAVE THREE GRANDCHILDREN—Leslie's son, Eric (born in 1972), and Jeannine's two children, David (born in 1993) and Johanna (born in 1999), better known as Josie.

During various periods of Eric's life, I was able to be more involved with him. For example, when as a pre-teen, he spent a weekend with me in Manhattan, I took him for lunch at the Windows on the World restaurant at the top of the World Trade Center. Like all of us he was horrified when on September 11, 2001, the World Trade Center was destroyed. He felt a personal attachment to it. He developed an interest in restaurants and has worked in several as an adult.

David exhibited an exceptional level of computer literacy as well as navigational skills. Jeannine counted on him to help with travel directions. He loved to peruse maps and travel guides and was an avid reader, including devouring all the Harry Potter books. He has a marvelous sense of humor, and he particularly enjoyed the Mr. Bean TV shows while he was growing up. He recognizes his limitations caused by Asperger's Syndrome and deals well with them. This is largely because of Jeannine's extensive research and understanding of the subject. She is able to guide him in learning how to balance his different-ness with the demands of school and everyday life.

Josie demonstrates remarkable musical and artistic talent. When she was only about nine years old I taught her how to play Beethoven's *Fur Elise* on the piano. She memorized it quickly. She pursued piano lessons for several years, and when she was twelve years old she played Beethoven's *Moonlight Sonata* from memory at a recital. Now in high school she sings, often solo, in the school chorus. She also paints beautifully in oil and watercolor. Mature far beyond her years, she is frequently mistaken for an adult. This has been a challenge for her, but she is coping with it well, again, with Jeannine's guidance and support. Jeannine matured quickly herself, so she knows how difficult that can be for a young girl.

I am grateful to live in Minnesota now enabling me to see Jeannine and her children often.

Chapter 14

Midlife Metamorphosis

BEGINNING IN THE 1970S, I embarked on a path of expanded spiritual exploration and psychological healing. I needed to reclaim who I was and develop a view of life that made sense to me.

My maternal grandmother and my parents practiced Christian Science, and my siblings and I were reared in this tradition. After Ernie and I were married, I had twice served as Second Reader in two small Christian Science churches—in Rolla, Missouri, during the late 1940s and again in the mid-1950s in Gainesville, Florida. But by 1976, the church organization had become patriarchal and hierarchal not by the founder—Mary Baker Eddy—but by the men who followed her and took over the Mother Church in Boston, which set the rules for all the branch churches. The men established dictatorial rules for membership: e.g., members must confine their reading on religion to publications issued by the Mother Church; and members must rely solely on Christian Science for physical healing and not seek any kind of help from medical doctors. I couldn't understand why the kind of healing prayer taught by Mary Baker Eddy would conflict with medical help. Dr. Larry Dossey successfully integrated the power of prayer with medicine and has illustrated well the mind-body connection in his books, *Meaning and Medicine* and *Healing Words*.

Like two of my brothers, who had long since left Christian Science, and Denise, who pursued a different approach, I felt the religion was not for me. While I continued to embrace some of the philosophy of Christian Science, the restrictions and impractical nature of the church's rules caused me to resign from membership. Apparently many others left the church as well, perhaps for the same reasons. In the 1930s, Christian Science church membership worldwide numbered 300,000; now it is only 61,000. Statistics compiled from the listings in the *Christian Science Journal*, an official church periodical, indicate a sharp decline in the number of churches and practitioners. In the United States alone, the number of practitioners has fallen from almost 5,000 in 1971 to 1,161 in 2005, and the number of churches has declined from 1,829 to 1,000 in the same period. Moreover, on Sunday mornings and Wednesday evening services, attendance is only a fraction of what it had been in the 1950s, 1960s, and 1970s.

Rather than becoming affiliated with any organized religion, I decided to pursue an independent study of spiritual traditions and practices, developing my own approach. My readings included books on shamanism as well as books on meditation practices, leading me to adopt regular periods of meditation in my routine.

My explorations included research on family systems—what makes them healthy and how and why they fall into dysfunctional patterns. This research helped me understand my own original family's dynamics and the emotional patterns I had developed in response. For example, like so many other children, to avoid being shamed for expressing anger or misbehaving, I sought to please my mother and to live up to her expectations for how her perfect little "Mary Joy" should behave. To do this, I had learned to suppress my own emotions, stuffing them deep inside. As an adult, I could not even cry. The message was that my mother considered who I was to be unacceptable and that, to be accepted, I had to become who she wanted me to be. That I should end up lacking self-esteem made sense to me. My low self-esteem had nothing to do with my real abilities or character; it was a response to early childhood experiences and the way my mother thought best to raise me.

So, in the mid 1980s, while working in Manhattan, I enrolled in an evening psychotherapy course for adult children of dysfunctional families. Therapist Donna Torbico conducted the class entitled, "Bottom Lines."

For the first time, I learned about healthy personal boundaries and boundary invasion (such as lack of privacy). When she talked about the child's need for unconditional love, I remembered my mother saying, "If you love me, you won't do that." I learned about childhood emotional wounding and abuse, such as shaming, about safe ways to express healthy anger, about emotional abandonment (not having your inner needs met during childhood), spiritual abandonment (demanding perfection and blind obedience, using "spiritual" statements to terrify a child—such as my mother saying "you're letting the devil talk to you"). The course also covered steps to pursue recovery and growth.

Then, in the late 1990s, I sought some one-on-one therapy from Linda Brackin in Delaware to supplement what I had learned in Donna Torbico's course. Linda helped me grow in every area of my life—emotionally, spiritually, socially, and even physically. Looking back on my life before I began this therapy, I feel that I had been mostly "in my head" and not fully present with my body, which I had been taught as a child to ignore. Linda guided me in bringing to closure—through writing and appropriate rituals—unfinished business, e.g., healing lingering wounds from childhood, especially around my relationship with my mother; wounds from a forty-year marriage; and persistent grief over Bill's tragic death in 1954. I also participated for a time in Linda's Inner Child support group.

Through this intentional work on myself, I felt freer of these and other issues that had weighed on me all my life. It became possible for me to express anger when appropriate and at last I could easily weep real tears. And my achievements in my career helped enormously in shifting my self-awareness. But the opportunity that Northeastern University Press offered me in 1995 to write a book—*Women Pioneers for the Environment*—boosted my self-esteem most of all.

I have come to believe that as women become self-assertive and do more activist organizing, we will be able to participate directly in decision-making or at least exercise greater influence on decisions. The world needs our wisdom, since women are focused on future generations. I believe women can make the difference in shifting our course away from corporate greed and control and the use of force to address our national interests—away from the military-industrial complex. In 2010, Kate Nustedt, UK executive director of Women for Women International, commented: "We all know by now that one woman can change anything and many women can change everything."[13]

During the 1980s, I expanded the scope of my personal, inner work and became interested in past-life regression. This field expanded my sense of who I was and what others were doing here—that we were here for purposes that had to do with our souls' growth. It also drove home the message that this life was not all there was. I obtained a couple past-life readings from a regression practitioner. While I still worked for Audubon in New York City, I took vacation time in the early 1990s to attend two conferences organized by the International Transpersonal Association, an organization based in California, founded by Czech-born medical doctor and psychiatrist, Dr. Stanislav Grof. At conferences in Prague, Czech Republic, in 1992, and in Killarney, Ireland, in 1994, I had the opportunity to learn about Dr. Grof's research on the human unconscious and nonordinary reality. Other sessions at these conferences featured speakers such as spiritual teacher and author Ram Dass; Jean Shinoda Bolen, a psychologist and author about positive archetypes for women in the third phase of their lives; Charles Tart, transpersonal psychologist and author about altered states of consciousness; innovative British biologist Rupert Sheldrake, who writes and lectures about his theory of morphic resonance; Richard Tarnas, cultural historian, author, and professor of philosophy and psychology; Kenneth Ring, researcher, writer and lecturer on near-death experiences; John Mack on the UFO abduction phenomenon; and Michael Harner on shamanism. This was an exciting, mind-expanding period for me, and it shifted my worldview.

After attending these conferences, I studied many of the books these thinkers and researchers have written. I also plunged into reading the

---

[13]Statement on September 7, 2010, after presenting a petition to UK Prime Minister David Cameron, calling for greater UN investment in women in war-torn countries to help them rebuild their lives and communities.

books of psychiatrist Raymond Moody about near-death experiences as well as physician and therapist Dr. Brian Weiss's works on past-life regression and reincarnation. Again, this literature expanded my sense of life—who we are, why we are here, and the nature of life—in ways that were experiential and concrete. I saw how the larger soul-story of a person's life could manifest in one's experiences here and now.

These explorations have led me to believe that my identity, my authentic selfhood, is a spiritual entity or soul and that I am currently having a human incarnation for purposes that relate to my larger development.

Approaching the experience of passing over does not frighten me. In fact, I'm curious about what it is like on the other side. Two of my brothers are already there, the eldest and the youngest of my siblings, Bill and John. I do hope, however, that the journey over will occur quickly without an extended incapacity or suffering. After all, who doesn't hope for that?

As I mentioned earlier, in 2009, I read a trilogy of books about the afterlife by Dr. Michael Newton, a hypnotherapist in California: *Journey of Souls*, *Destiny of Souls*, and *Life Between Lives*. The third book reveals Dr. Newton's step-by-step methods. During three or four-hour sessions, Dr. Newton takes his hypnosis clients beyond their past life memories to explore their deep memories of what they experienced as souls between lives. I must confess I found what his clients reported absolutely fascinating, and the accounts have stayed with me ever since. Apparently, many others have responded this way too. His first book, *Journey of Souls*, has sold more than 200,000 copies and has been translated into ten languages.

Throughout the decades of my spiritual research and psychological therapy, regular discussions with my philosopher daughter, Denise, have encouraged me and enhanced my spiritual growth and understanding.

Along these lines, I have always found a poem by Irish author Violet Hay (1873 to 1969) inspiring.

> From sense to Soul my pathway lies before me.
> From mist and shadow into Truth's clear day;
> The dawn of all things real is breaking o'er me,
> My heart is singing: I have found the way.

I reach Mind's open door, and at its portal
I know that where I stand is holy ground;
I feel the calm and joy of things immortal,
The loveliness of Love is all around.

The way leads upward and its goal draws nearer,
Thought soars enraptured, fetterless and free;
The vision infinite to me grows clearer,
I touch the fringes of eternity.

Chapter 15

Dwelling Dramas and Joys

THE DWELLING PLACES WE OCCUPY during our lives often hold unforeseen surprises—sometimes shocking, sometimes disappointing, sometimes resulting in a gold mine. In fact, one of my abodes, a tiny one-room apartment I occupied for ten years in mid-Manhattan, brought me a small fortune, which I will explain later.

During my eighty-plus years, I have moved more than twenty times, lived in nine different states—all but one of which (my birthplace, Minneapolis) were east of the Mississippi River. During the first decade of our marriage, Ernie and I moved ten times.

So far in this book, I have written about the bungalow where I was born in Minneapolis that we lost in a sheriff's sale; the crude shoebox in Eden Prairie that sheltered our family during the Great Depression; the basement apartment in Rolla, Missouri, that almost killed me; and the house across the highway from a major manure composing operation in Chester County, Pennsylvania.

Of all the other places I have lived, several stand out as favorites. One was an enchanting Carriage House on an old estate that we first rented in 1968. We eventually bought the house, which was nestled in a wooded area on Fells Lane in suburban Wilmington, Delaware.

This renovated historic stone structure, originally built in 1894, exuded charm and a unique character. It had arched Palladian windows, several with colored glass and most with deep window seats, as well as a split door in the kitchen, which was the original horse stable. The living room had once housed carriages. One bedroom upstairs had originally been the

Our Carriage House in suburban Wilmington, Delaware.

hayloft. It featured French doors with a half-circle fan window of colored glass above the doors. The master bedroom had exposed rustic ceiling rafters, and it had originally served as the first occupant's violin repair shop. Our three daughters finished growing up in this home.

During my seventeen years in this dwelling, we engaged in a succession of home improvement projects. Denise, Jeannine, and I created a rock garden near the walled-in patio off the kitchen. Inspired by the scene of a Russian field of daffodils in the film *Doctor Zhivago*, we planted over a hundred daffodil bulbs that offered a beautiful showcase view from our kitchen window each spring. We landscaped with a couple holly trees, a Japanese maple tree, and with rhododendron and azalea shrubs around the foundation.

Our field of daffodils behind the Carriage House.

The kitchen begged for redecorating. The long narrow all-white room with high ceiling and a giant fluorescent ceiling fixture reminded me of a sterile hospital clinic, totally incompatible with the over-all flavor of the Carriage House. After developing a plan, estimating cost, and procuring materials and equipment, I undertook the job of contractor myself, engaging subcontractors and supervising the labor. With the help of a Brazilian immigrant named Julio, a flamboyant handyman who greeted me each afternoon with much hand-kissing and bowing, we plunged in. Ernie had told him I would be the "job boss." He had never worked for a woman before. I had to prove myself.

Earlier experience with woodworking and other crafts had given me skills that I easily transferred to the project. I ended up teaching Julio, among other things, how to lay floor tile. As I wrote to a friend at the time, "I've been up to my neck in paint pots, stain sealers, junction boxes, sabre saws, rasps, chisels, expansion bolts, etc. Perhaps a career as a plumber or carpenter might have been more lucrative than secretarial work."

By introducing a burnt-orange counter top to give the room some glow, changing the lighting, rearranging the cupboards and appliances, lowering

Me in our Carriage House kitchen.

Above: the one-time Carriage House hayloft converted to a study. At left: The remodeled kitchen of our Carriage House.

the ceiling's appearance by installing artificial beams, we visually broadened the room. In the end, Julio proposed that he and I establish a home remodeling business partnership.

Once all the children had flown the nest, I converted the room that had been the original hayloft into a study, using unfinished furniture I sanded, stained, and finished with shellac. This study served as a weekend retreat where I began researching and collecting material that in 1995 eventually—and, as I explained, unexpectedly—led to my writing, *Women Pioneers for the Environment*.

By the mid 1980s, it became apparent that, without the help of my daughters, trying to maintain this large suburban house and property involved more time and effort than I could manage while working in New York City during the week. At the same time, my marriage situation had become bleak.

I learned that a friend wanted to sell her shares in Rodney Court, a historic cooperative apartment building on Pennsylvania Avenue in Wilmington, Delaware. The building—named after Cesar Rodney, Delaware's signer of the Declaration of Independence—was listed on the National Register. Ernie agreed to help me purchase the co-op shares as a rental "investment." I wanted to move into the apartment. He claimed he could not tolerate living in an apartment. "The only way I'll ever leave the Carriage House is in a coffin."

"Isn't that a rather rigid position?" I retorted.

In 1985, I moved into the spacious third-floor apartment in Rodney Court, furnishing it by using a bequest left to me by my Uncle Fremont. The elegant apartment, the largest in the building, had originally been custom designed for a DuPont family member. It had more square feet than my current bungalow in St. Paul and featured an entry hall, large living and dining rooms, a music or library alcove off the living room, a breakfast room with a built-in buffet, a kitchen with walk-in pantry, three bedrooms, two full baths, and seven closets. Wow!

Through the process of sorting where we each wanted to live, Ernie and I agreed to go our separate ways. He stayed in the Carriage House for a while. But he soon remarried, and he ended up living in a series of apartments and condominiums after all. He rented the Carriage House for quite a few years, eventually selling it and giving me my equity in the property.

* * * *

EVEN THOUGH OUR DAUGHTERS HAD grown up and were living on their own, I continued to come back to Wilmington on the weekends. I enjoyed the more peaceful life and pace of Wilmington compared with New York City. And I wanted to see my daughters, all of whom still lived in Wilmington then. One experience stands out in my mind from this period. Simple as it is, I will never forget it.

143

One Saturday, a friend and I were having lunch at the Columbus Inn on Pennsylvania Avenue in Wilmington, not far from my Rodney Court apartment. The sound of her velvet voice floated across the dining room to me from two tables away.

"I know that voice," I said to my lunch companion. "It's Maya Angelou." I looked over to where the voice came from and recognized her from the side view of her face. I wanted to speak to her but hesitated out of respect for the privacy celebrities cherish but seldom experience. I wanted her to know how much I admired her. What to do?

"Who's Maya Angelou?" my friend asked. "I've never heard of her." As an avid Clinton supporter, I felt sure he'd remember that she'd written a special poem for the newly elected president entitled, "On the Pulse of the Morning," which she delivered at his 1993 Inaugural Ceremony.

"I don't remember that," he said. "Tell me more."

So I did.

"Well, Clinton described her as his favorite living poet. In 1971, she received a Pulitzer Prize nomination for one of her poems, 'Just Give Me a Cool Drink of Water 'fore I Die.' She's a highly acclaimed author. So far, she's published ten best-selling books, most of them autobiographical. I remember being deeply moved when I read her first book, *I Know Why the Caged Bird Sings*. It's an account of her growing-up years to age seventeen in the segregated South, and it's her most widely acclaimed book. She abandoned her real name—Marguerite Annie Johnson—and adopted the nickname her brother, whom she adored, gave her—'Maya,' which means 'my' or 'mine.' Her last name—Angelou—came from the name of one of her husbands—Tosh Angelos—a sailor of Greek descent.

"When she was seven years old and living with her mother in St. Louis, her birthplace," I continued, "her divorced mother's boyfriend raped her. At the rapist's trial, Maya was forced to testify. Several days later, the police found the rapist beaten to death. In her child's mind, Maya thought her words at the trial had a connection with the man's death, so she resolved to stop talking. 'I thought if I spoke, anybody might die,' she said. Her mother sent her back to Stamps, Arkansas, to live with her paternal grandmother. She spoke to no one for nearly six years. Later in life, she remarked that during that period, she believed her whole body was an ear."

"Goodness," said my friend, "what a depressing story."

"It gets better," I assured him. "Her life became stellar. She started her career in drama and dance—performing folk, blues, and calypso gigs in New York City clubs—but she soon moved on to other things. And in every medium she chose—as poet, author, journalist, historian, civil rights activist, screenwriter, playwright, actress, producer or director—she broke ground for women of color. Her screenplay, Georgia, Georgia was the first screenplay by a black woman to be filmed. She had a role in a production of Porgy and Bess, which toured internationally for almost a year. I remember seeing her star with Winona Ryder several years ago in a movie entitled Making an American Quilt.

"Do you remember the TV series, Roots?" I asked my friend.

"Oh, yes," he said. "a compelling television series."

"Well, Maya Angelou was nominated for an Emmy Award for her portrayal of the grandmother of Kunta Kinte, the central character.

"She's also a scholar and teacher," I said, "and the recipient of many honorary degrees. She speaks French, Spanish, Arabic, and West African Fanti. One of her several marriages was to a South African freedom fighter.

"When she was living in Cairo, she became editor of a weekly called The Arab Observer, the only English-language news weekly in the Middle East. In Ghana, she served The African Review as feature editor and taught at the University of Ghana."

"Wow," my companion exclaimed. "I can't believe I've never heard of her."

"There's more," I said. "During the 1960s, Martin Luther King recruited her to be the northern coordinator for the Southern Christian Leadership Conference. In the 1970s, President Gerald Ford appointed her to the Bicentennial Commission. President Jimmy Carter persuaded her to serve on the National Commission for the Observance of International Women's Year.

"Like you," I said, "she's a habitual early riser, awakening each morning at 5:00 a.m. I read that she goes to a motel room near her home every morning, taking a Bible, a thesaurus, a dictionary, and a bottle of sherry. Stretching out on the bed, she writes with pencil on a yellow pad."

"I can understand why you admire her so much," my friend said. "Are you going to muster enough courage to speak to her?"

"Well, I don't know. I don't want to intrude on her privacy. But I tell you what—I think I'll just write her a brief note."

Dredging up a scrap of paper from my handbag, I wrote, "Dear Maya Angelou, Many thanks for your splendid contributions over the years to the world's literature and performing arts."

Then came the hard part. How will I give it to her without being intrusive? Finally I stood up, walked over, touched her shoulder lightly and silently slipped the note under the right edge of her plate.

After she read my note, she looked over at me and smiled.

When my friend and I were almost finished with our meal, I became aware of a commanding six-foot presence standing beside our table. It was Maya Angelou. I remembered how a *New York Times* writer had once described her: "Her features are broad, like chunks of clay collected roughly on a frame. Her hands are large, her mouth a cut of red across her face. Even her laugh seems big. But she has the innate and compelling grace of a woman who has constructed a full life, one lived without concession or false excuse."[14]

She smiled graciously, placed a hand-written note on our table beside me, and walked away. The note said, "Mary Joy! Breton, Joy! Thank you for your kind words, Maya Angelou, 10/19/97."

Happy day! I beamed, feeling deeply honored.

* * * *

FOR FIFTEEN YEARS I ENJOYED living in Rodney Court. During the first ten years, I continued to work in Manhattan during the workweek, maintaining an apartment there also. After I retired from Audubon in 1995, the last five years in Rodney Court found me totally occupied

---

[14]Catherine S. Manegold, "An Afternoon with Maya Angelou, a Wordsmith at Her Inaugural Anvil," *The New York Times*, January 20, 1993.

with researching and writing *Women Pioneers for the Environment*, followed by promotional travel and talks for the book.

Rodney Court turned out to be a lucrative financial investment. When I sold my shares in 2000, their value had tripled.

*   *   *   *

TO DESCRIBE MY NEW YORK EXPERIENCE, I must go back to 1979 when the opportunity to work at the National Audubon Society headquarters arose. Obviously, how I was going to handle my living arrangement if I took the job posed the biggest question. Did I want to live in New York City during the workweek? My first reaction, "I don't think so." But friends urged me to give it a try. "You'll love New York." At least it would be a broadening experience, so I agreed.

As it turned out, I *did* love being in Manhattan. With superb public transportation available, good walking shoes, and a city map in hand, learning to get around the city proved easy and fun.

My studio apartment at Fifty-fourth and Second Avenue, Manhattan, 1951.

My first pad was a tiny studio on the top (fifth) floor of a building at 254 East Fifty-fourth Street (corner of Second Avenue). The apartment overlooked David's Chocolate Chip Cookies shop across the street and was four blocks north of Kathryn Hepburn's town house. She was an icon in my early movie-going days, and so I made sure I attended Hepburn's last stage play appearance, *West Side Waltz*, in 1981.

Riding the "E" subway train to Penn Station each Friday to catch the Amtrak Metroliner to Wilmington for the weekend offered an experience unlike any other. In my journal, here's what I wrote about it in 1982.

"Train already full when it stopped at Lexington and Third. Large crowd waiting on platform. I was swept/pressed into the jammed car. Bodies squashed together. No need to hold on to pole or overhead rod, even if I could reach one. I couldn't have fallen down. Being short, my face at armpit height of men next to me who were hanging onto overhead rod. Body odors stifling. Wrong time to have a hot flash, but I did. Very hot in the car—so many bodies packed in. Could feel the buttocks of those around me smashed up against me."

One Friday afternoon while waiting on the platform for the "E" train, an African-American woman approached me. "Is this your wrist watch?" Indeed it was. I hadn't felt it fall off my wrist, but this kind woman had seen it drop and picked it up. The watch was a treasured memento I had invested in to remind me of my New York experience— a $500 Tiffany watch with a small sapphire in the stem! Wow. "Bless your heart. Thank you a million times."

What did I like about living in New York? Concerts at Lincoln Center, especially *Mostly Mozart* every summer; visiting Rockefeller Center; walking in Central Park, relaxing in Green Acre vest-pocket park on Fifty-first Street with its waterfall—a park created by Abby Rockefeller in 1971; meals at the Russian Tea Room next to Carnegie Hall or the Brasserie on special occasions with visiting family or friends; the New York Public Library; museums, especially exhibits at the Metropolitan Museum of Art; the Union Square Farmers' Market; attending events at the New York Open Center in Greenwich Village and at the Omega Institute in Rhinebeck, a scenic train ride up the Hudson river from the City. I liked the small French bakeries, the aroma of baked goods drifting out onto the street; the small fruit and vegetable stands, the flower shops. Sometimes I would go have lunch at the World Trade Towers. And, of course, I loved going to plays on Broadway. Taking Jeannine to see *Cats* at the Wintergarden Theatre became a peak experience for both of us. Andrew Lloyd Webber's signature piece *Memories* remains a favorite.

What didn't I like? Mostly sensory experiences bothered me: bad odors, such as stale urine floating from an alley; the sight of litter everywhere, often swirling in the wind around the skyscrapers; and the noise level on the street, which I think contributed to my hearing impairment. Even after I had worked in New York a number of years, the litter still bothered me. People claimed I would get used to it, but I didn't. I wanted to get out my broom and dustpan and clean up the sidewalks. NYC could be so beautiful with cleaner streets and more window boxes of flowers. That was surely my mother's influence coming out.

Sometimes I walked the four blocks from work to my Fifty-fourth Street apartment as late as 11:00 p.m. The streets would still be teeming with people and taxis. New York never goes to sleep completely. Once home, after washing my face while preparing for bed, I noticed the washcloth bore telltale evidence of the city's air pollution.

It took me almost a year to learn to sleep through the big city noises—whining garbage trucks, police and ambulance sirens, rumbling trucks. I wore ear-plugs for months.

*   *   *   *

IN 1985, SIX YEARS AFTER I had signed a lease for the one-room apartment on East Fifty-fourth Street, the landlord decided to raze the building and erect a luxury high-rise in its place. By law, the landlord could not then evict tenants, raise their rent, or renew leases. The tenants organized an association and retained an attorney on consignment to represent our interests. One by one over the next five years, the attorney negotiated lease buy-out deals for tenants as they made plans to move out. I stayed in my apartment until only one other tenant and I remained in the building.

Little did I realize how wise a decision that turned out to be. In October 1989, the landlord bought out my lease for $525,000. Over half a million! Wow!

Out of that, I had to pay the attorney's fee, which was twenty-five percent or $132,000. And, of course, I had to pay federal income tax and New York State income tax, which ate up another huge hunk—over $100,000.

In the end, my net settlement amounted to a bit over $250,000. But what a windfall!

I wrote generous checks to my daughters and invested the remain-

Scenic Roosevelt Island in East River, Manhattabn.

My Roosevelt Island apartment.

The Roosevelt Island Aerial Tramway.

der in mutual funds. This stroke of luck enabled me to underwrite Denise's Idea House publishing venture and the production of her first book, *The Soul of Economies: Spiritual Evolution Goes to the Marketplace.* Together, we learned all about the book-publishing world. Much as the industry has changed due to technology, this experience laid the foundation for our work today with Living Justice Press. That windfall made my life today possible in another way. In 2000, I redeemed some of the mutual funds to make the down payment on the bungalow I bought in St. Paul, Minnesota, where Denise and I now live and work.

After this lease buy-out, in the fall of 1989, I rented a one-bedroom apartment on the eleventh floor of Manhattan Park, a new residential building on Roosevelt Island, a sliver of land in the East River two miles long and 800 feet across, midway between Manhattan and Queens. My apartment overlooked the west channel of the East River with a view of Manhattan in the background.

The flavor of Roosevelt Island resembles a small, tranquil village. It is resplendent with parks, grassy open spaces, promenades, flowering trees, a lighthouse, playing fields for sports, restaurants, plus shops along its (one and only) Main Street. Roosevelt Island is a four-minute ride by aerial tramway to Fifty-ninth Street and Second Avenue in Manhattan, a great fun ride, as long as the weather cooperates. The tram closes during thunderstorms. About the time I took up residence, a subway link also opened.

The day I moved into this new dwelling, my unpacking became continually interrupted by my watching boats go by on the river—tugboats, sailboats, speedboats, the Circle Tour boat, motorboats, fishing boats, barges, schooners, sloops, yachts, cargo ships, tankers—a fascinating array.

And my small balcony provided an opportunity to enjoy planting a few potted impatiens. As one can well imagine, living on Roosevelt Island during the workweek ranks high among my favorite dwelling places. I spent the final six years of my Audubon tenure there.

*   *   *   *

MY CURRENT DWELLING IS a small one-and-a-half story arts and crafts bungalow in St. Paul that dates back to 1925, built a year after my birth. In 2007, Denise and I added a three-season porch to the back of the house, replacing a charming arbor and deck that had finally succumbed to rot and had become rodent habitat.

Gardening for me immediately became an enjoyable feature of this place. Minnesota has a short growing season, but come May, people's gardens and window boxes burst forth with beauty and an abundance of flowers. Lilacs, petunias, geraniums, impatiens, iris, peonies, black-eyed Susans, and phlox are a few that seem to be among people's favorites. When all the lilacs bloom in May, their fragrance effuses the entire city.

Among the collection of houseplants on our back porch, a direct descendant of a different kind from my mother occupies a special spot in the sun. A desert plant, a night-blooming cereus, evolved from a slip Jeannine had originally taken from my mother's plant. Several years ago Jeannine gave us a slip from her plant. Ours hasn't bloomed yet, but we're giving it

Our St. Paul bungalow.

Our Juliet Avenue bungalow, St. Paul.

Leslie (left), and Denise holding bloosom of night-blooming cereus, in my mother's garden in Winter Haven, Florida, 1961.

The back yard of our Juliet Avenue home.

Border gardenbeds at juliet Avenue home.

TLC with hopes that we will be rewarded in time. The fragrant and spectacular blossoms unfold rapidly at night, and are dazzling to watch, but the blooms last only one day in summer. Jeannine said that when hers bloomed, the blossom attracted moths and other creatures she had not seen before.

Denise and I operate our tiny nonprofit publishing venture—Living Justice Press—from our home. Our dining room table serves as "Living Justice Press Central." We warehouse most of our book inventory in our basement where we also operate a book-packing center and store filing cabinets for our non-current records. We created an office in one of the bedrooms on the main floor where we conduct computer research and promotion work, LJP bill-paying, and processing checks from book sales for depositing in the bank.

Denise has a computer work-station in an alcove of her upstairs quarters. As executive director, she does extensive editing of each manuscript, prepares indexes, oversees production and printing, and performs innumerable administrative functions, including fund-raising and public relations as well as processing orders and hauling books to the post office. Sometimes she sets up an exhibit table at a local conference

Portrait of me (left) in 1999. Denise and me (right) at an event about LJP's books at the Saint Catherine University, St. Paul, October 2003.

and sells our titles. We hold our nonprofit's quarterly Board meetings in our enclosed back porch.

This Juliet Avenue bungalow in St. Paul has me pretty much settled in, I believe, for the duration of my life. The Twin Cities area is where I began my journey on Earth, and it seems fitting to conclude it here.

Chapter 16

Hobbies

S ITTING IN THE MIDDLE of the living room floor of our first bare rental apartment in Riverton, New Jersey, in 1950, I studied the space around me, envisioning the items of furniture we would need. Our crawling youngster, Leslie, jabbered as she explored the empty rooms on her hands and knees. I grabbed her as she passed by, changing her soiled diaper on the floor.

During the early years of our marriage, when my husband, Ernie, attended college after World War II, utilizing the "G. I. Bill of Rights." we had lived in furnished apartments, we did not own one stick of furniture.

So off I went to various junk shops and used-furniture stores, seeking the bare essentials—a table and chairs, a box bed, a dresser, a sofa, and a couple lamps for a start. But the bare floor in the living room loomed cold and stark. What to do for a rug?

Since most of our second-hand acquisitions turned out to be early American in character, a braided rug seemed appropriate. However, the cost of a hand-made braided rug was prohibitive, and machine-made ones did not appeal to me. So I decided to make one myself.

At this point, my mother, famous for her frugality, wrote to me from Minnesota: "I've been saving woolen garments for decades for just such an enterprise, but I've never been able to take time to undertake such a project." She gladly shipped them off to me for a rug.

Her accumulation included clothing worn variously by everyone in our family. As I cut them up in two-inch-wide strips of varying lengths, I recognized such items as suits and trousers worn by my father and three

My braided rug, with Leslie, 1952.

brothers, skirts and coats that had been mine. I hugged each piece to my face, breathing in its essence of long ago. Even the woolen leg wraps from my father's World War I Army uniform were among the collection.

After deciding on an autumn color scheme, I sorted the materials and had a few dyed.

Folding the raw edges of the strips to the inside as I braided three strands together, I staggered the terminal points, overlapping and stitching on additional bias-cut strips as I went along. Staggering the lengths and bias-cutting the strips made the braiding smooth and uniform in thickness. The braiding process and then hand sewing the braid to the rug core took place alternately. Easing the braid around the curve at each end of the oval rug to prevent its curling up proved a bit tricky.

As the rug increased in size, it became necessary to sit on the floor to work on it.

When all the woolen material initially at hand had been used up, the rug was still not large enough to suit me. Surreptitiously, I began ransacking our closets for garments I might seize upon for the project. Ernie's World War II uniforms finally fell prey to my scissors. I felt sure he would never need them again. But, just our luck, within a matter of weeks after the uniforms had become an integral part of the rug, Ernie

158

was called back to active duty as a reserve officer in the Army Air Force during the Korean War.

At last, the rug was finished, after a year of working on it.

The rug became one of the first things guests noticed and inquired about. And it was not at all unusual for me to be on my hands and knees with friends pointing out pieces of material, "And these were my father's *World War I* Army uniform leg wraps. This was a skirt I wore as a child, and these pieces were my brothers' trousers." And, of course, Ernie's comment was always: "And *these* are my Army Air Force uniforms that she cut up two weeks before I was called back to active duty."

*   *   *   *

SO WITH THIS AMBITIOUS INITIAL PROJECT, rug-making became one of my hobbies. Casting about for other rug-making options, over the years I chose a succession of four hand-hooked wool rug kits. With the rug canvas draped over a card table in a corner of our dining room in the Carriage House, I sat hooking the rug while we all watched television: the Huntley-Brinkley and Walter Cronkite evening news programs on weeknights and on Sunday evenings Masterpiece Theater's *Upstairs-Downstairs* and then the *Poldark* series. Denise often took a turn with the hooking.

Managing a home afforded me all kinds of opportunities for creative expression. Interior decorating alone generated a plethora of projects in addition to making rugs: draperies, slip covers, dust-ruffle skirts for beds, embroidered wall hangings, quilt-making, and furniture refinishing, not to mention cooking and gardening.

During pregnancies, I felt compelled to do embroidering. First, I did several traditional samplers. Then, when I was pregnant with Denise, I undertook embroidering a set of six antique cars. Afterward I framed them using monk's cloth-covered cardboard to create mats. Today these six wall hangings decorate one wall in our home office.

During my pregnancy with Jeannine, I began embroidering a cross-stitched "Friendship" design quilt top, double-bed size. Jeannine remembers playing house under the quilting frame we set up temporarily in our living room to do the quilting once the embroidered top was finished.

We used the finished quilt on our bed for several years. But this ill-fated quilt met with disaster. When I began working out of town during the week, I packed it away in a cardboard carton in our storage room at the Carriage House. Unfortunately, mice invaded the box, eating holes in the quilt, seeking the cotton batting inner filling for nesting. (In hindsight a wiser storage choice would have been a cedar chest.) In addition, the red embroidery floss faded and deteriorated to the point that the cross-stitching fell apart. The red embroidery floss that came with the quilt kit must have been of inferior quality, because I have an all-red antique cross-stitched sampler made in the mid 1860s by Alta Parker, the daughter of my grandmother's sister, Belle. The sampler depicts an oriental scene of a boy flying a kite near a pagoda. The red embroidery floss Alta used remains brilliant and flawless. Alta's framed sampler hangs over a writing desk in my bedroom.

The remains of my irreparably damaged cross-stitched quilt lie folded up in a cedar chest in our basement here in St. Paul. I don't know what to do with it.

Jeannine sitting on the log cabin quilt, playing her guitar.

Another quilt project proved more successful. Using scraps of cotton left over from years of making clothes for everyone in the family, I created a log-cabin design quilt for Jeannine's trundle bed at the Carriage House.

Early on in our marriage, I learned to refinish used furniture, including chair seat caning and rushing. I did this of necessity, since this was the least expensive route to furnish our first dwellings. I had fun doing this, as with the other hobbies. About the time I began pursuing the refinishing, a non-toxic water-soluble paint and varnish stripper became available, making the process safer and easier. Among the pieces I refinished and still have are a small spindle-backed Arts-and-Crafts cane-seated chair with a hand-carved top rail, a chair that had lain in pieces for many years in my grand-mother's attic and that had to be stripped of paint and reassembled; a rock maple hutch cabinet and drop-leaf table; and a rock maple coffee table that I cobbled together from a discarded kitchen table I found in the Car-riage House garage soon after we moved in.

* * * *

PERHAPS THE LONGEST SUSTAINED CRAFT hobby that engaged me was sewing. I sewed my first dress when I was twelve years old without the benefit of any Home-Ec guidance—only advice from my busy mother. My biggest mistake? Selecting a pattern that featured bound buttonholes down the entire front. Oh, boy, why didn't anyone warn me? Influenced by my mother's industriousness and rules about "waste not, want not," I managed to finish the dress. Surprisingly, I wore it with some pride in spite of its obvious flaws. But I concluded that sewing was not for me.

It wasn't until several years after marriage that I tried again. Ernie bought a small portable sewing machine. He believed all households needed one for mending, if nothing else. But once we had the machine, I developed a keen desire to learn to sew. Living a good distance from a city where I might have taken lessons, I taught myself with the help of sewing books, pattern directions, and kind neighbors.

The meaning of sewing terms such as slip stitch, catch stitch, pinking, piping, facings, darts, and yokes escaped me. Nevertheless, I plunged in and soon developed such a passion for sewing that the first Christmas after acquiring the machine, I made gifts for everyone on our list: men's sports shirts (I cut two left sleeves and no right one the first time around); embroidered felt handbags, billfolds, stuffed toys, embroidered potholders, and aprons. Creating stuffed toys for the children offered the most fun: for example, Raggedy Ann and Andy dolls and Humpty Dumpty. Jeannine still has them. I also made elf tree ornaments.

Following pattern instructions, I managed to translate what at first seemed like Greek into directions I could understand and follow. I learned not to be concerned about the steps far ahead, but to execute them one at a time. When I progressed to the point that at the outset had seemed impossible to understand, the steps to take next became clear.

A major motive in undertaking sewing in my case was to create a wardrobe of quality and quantity that I couldn't afford to buy ready made.

During the years when parenting and home management occupied me full time, I squeezed in moments to make more clothes than I had occasions in which to wear them. Later, after resuming an outside career, I needed a larger wardrobe, but had much less time available to sew.

Raggedy Ann and Andy dolls I made.

I learned over my years of sewing that the finished garment seldom matched my expectations for it. The more successful outfits were often ones I was not especially enthusiastic about initially. And only a few could be described as elegant. Sewing clothes is a bit of a gamble. You can't try the dress or suit on before you begin. Even if you make a muslin mock-up (as the pattern occasionally suggested), you can't tell the way the finished piece will look or how comfortable it will be. I did my best to be a good sport about the few duds I produced. And it seemed I was always a season behind in creating even a minimum wardrobe. While I chose fairly classic designs, there is only so much hem one can build into a garment to accommodate ever-fluctuating hemlines.

Even using the precise fabrics and patterns shown in pattern fashion photos didn't always bring satisfying results. Once I hit on a skirt pattern that fitted me well and looked good, I used it over and over for years, scotch-taping together the shreds of the tissue pattern, using it through fashion cycles that dictated skirt length from mid-calf to above the knee and then back to mid-calf. Similarly I re-used many times over a classic tailored women's shirt pattern making cotton, silk, or soft wool shirts, several of which I still wear today, thirty years or more later. For sure, each of my hand-tailored garments could be considered an "original" insofar as the combinations of fabric and pattern are concerned.

At one point, I spent a long time creating a carefully tailored sport jacket for Ernie. But he never wore it. It ended up in the Good Will collection. The problem: the fabric choice. A high-pressure salesman in a fabric store persuaded me it would be "one of a kind." It certainly became that all right. Obviously, he wanted to move his inventory.

Once I became economically independent with a well-paying job, I invested in quality clothes without feeling guilty.

One Saturday morning, probably around 1993, within an hour's time at a high quality store, I spent over $300 for five dresses—precisely the therapy I needed and worth every penny. A few days earlier, I had rolled up and chucked into the Good Will bag—without ever wearing it—a designer-pattern dress on which I had worked an hour or so each evening for several weeks. The pattern looked chic in the photograph in the pattern catalogue, but when I tried it on, it made me look fat (I then weighed about 110 pounds) and dowdy. It looked "homemade," not "custom tailored." It felt uncomfortable and had absolutely no pizzazz.

So after twenty-five years of making practically all my own clothes, I decided to declare an indeterminate moratorium on sewing.

Since retiring from a full-time job I need few clothes, so the moratorium still holds.

*   *   *   *

OF COURSE NONFICTION WRITING has been a life-long interest, more than a hobby actually, culminating in my writing the stories in this autobiography about my life experiences.

Chapter 17

Travel Tales

S TOP! STOP! WAAAIT! WAAAIT!" I shrieked as I raced along Fifty-ninth Street on foot chasing the taxicab. But the driver floored the accelerator and in seconds shot out of sight around the next corner into the darkness, taking with him my suitcase before I could retrieve it from the cab's back seat.

In the spring of 1995 I flew back to JFK Airport after a memorable weeklong holiday in Paris with my artist friend, Betty Collins, and several other friends. I had never before visited Paris. We stayed at a modest hotel near the Eiffel Tower and did all the usual touristy sight-seeing: finding the Sorbonne in the Latin Quarter, taking the elevator to the top of the Eiffel Tower, touring the Louvre and Rodin museums, visiting Notre Dame Cathedral, and Montmartre—the hill section of Paris where artists hang out—and walking down the Champs Elysee, not to mention taking a boat trip along the River Seine and eating in French bistros.

One day, a friend and I wandered into Printemps, a famous Paris department store. While there, we attended a fashion show. Later, as I strolled alone down one of the store's aisles, my eyes fell on a large square Yves Saint Laurent blue paisley cashmere scarf. I had a modest collection of silk and wool scarves and wore one almost every day. So I stopped to admire this cashmere scarf—the most beautiful one I have ever seen. I lingered at that counter a long time, entranced by the softness of the cashmere, captivated by the blue paisley design, wanting to buy it, thinking what a lovely memento it would be of my Paris vacation.

"*Ceci est magnifique, combien est ceci*—in dollars?" I finally asked.

"Five hundred thirty dollars," she responded.

"*Merci.*"

Gulp. "Well, that settles that," I muttered to myself as I stepped away. I had never spent that much on myself for any item—clothes or anything else. I felt guilty even contemplating the possibility.

My friends and I gathered for lunch in a Printemps restaurant, the one featuring a magnificent multicolored 1923 "Art Nouveau" cupola. I struggled not to think about the scarf.

That night, unable to sleep because of my roommate's snoring, I lay awake mentally visualizing the scarf. *What's come over me*, I wondered. I have never before experienced such an obsession.

Passing a pharmacy in the morning, I stopped in to buy some earplugs.

"*Bonjour, monsieur,*" I venture with my high school French, "*Excusez-moi, J'ai un probleme. Parlez-vous anglais?*"

"Try me," he replied.

Laying my head sideways on clasped hands, indicating sleep, I asked, "ear plugs?"

In seconds he produced a set, "*Merci, beaucoup.*"

That night I slept a bit better.

The day before we were to fly back to New York City, I decided to return to the department store "just to see if the scarf was still there." I prayed that it would not be, hoping fervently that someone else had purchased it so that I couldn't possibly be tempted. But the scarf was still there. After deliberating with myself for an agonizing fifteen or twenty minutes, and with a palpitating heart, I bought the scarf, charging it to my VISA credit card. On returning to our hotel room, I folded it carefully into my suitcase.

Back in New York, I took a bus from JFK airport to the Port Authority Bus Terminal. From there, I hailed a taxicab to take me to the Roosevelt Island aerial tramway plaza at Fifty-ninth and Second Avenue.

* * * *

After unsuccessfully chasing the taxi on foot, I just froze on the spot, stunned, puzzled, totally discombobulated. What to think? What to do? "Surely the driver would soon notice my suitcase on the back seat and swing back around to return it to me." So I just stood there rooted to the sidewalk, waiting for him to return. After some time when he did not appear, I boarded the aerial tramway and returned to my apartment on Roosevelt Island.

I could scarcely believe that the taxi driver had stolen my suitcase. From his appearance and his foreign language conversation on the taxi radio phone, I entertained the delusion that he was a religious and, therefore, honest person I could trust. My name, address, and telephone number were on the luggage tag. "Soon he will come by my apartment building and leave my bag with the concierge." Another false hope.

Eventually, I came to the inevitable realization that the driver had indeed deliberately swiped my suitcase. Mentally I replayed how it happened. After paying him, I had said, "Will you please wait a minute while I go around to the sidewalk side of the taxi to take my suitcase off the back seat?" When he didn't respond, I thought perhaps he had not understood what I said, so I repeated it. As I alighted from the taxi on the street side of the vehicle, I slammed the taxi door behind me. Apparently that was his cue. He took off like a shot. And, I must admit in hindsight, I acted not only as an "accomplice" but even an enabler of the crime.

Exhausted from the trans-Atlantic flight and suffering from jet lag, I had failed to do any of the right things when riding in a taxi. I had not made note of the taxi number on his dashboard I.D. tag or his name. After he sped off into the dark, it was impossible to take down the vehicle license number, even if I had had a pencil and pad at the ready. Worst of all, I had committed the cardinal mistake of paying him before stepping out of the taxi and before removing all my belongings.

Once inside my apartment, I collapsed on my sofa and just fell apart. Shaking and feeling totally devastated, I dissolved into tears. My beautiful new scarf, charged to my VISA, and so carefully folded in that suitcase, hadn't even been paid for yet.

I called the New York City Taxi and Limousine Commission to report the incident, relating my tale of woe to a sympathetic woman named Frances. With no clues to go on, however, she could do nothing. I also registered a report with the Police Property Clerk's Office at the Seventeenth Police Precinct as well as to the Port Authority Bus Terminal Police. All to no avail.

Shortly after I arrived back at my apartment, Denise called me from Delaware. She knew my travel schedule and was checking in.

"You'll never believe what just happened," I sobbed, telling her my miserable story. Feeling guilty I added, "I guess it serves me right for being selfish and self-indulgent enough to spend that kind of money on myself."

"Nonsense!" she insisted, "I'm delighted that your feelings of self-worth have finally developed to a level that allows you to invest in something beautiful for yourself. In fact," she added, "I think you should go right back to Paris and find another Yves Saint Laurent scarf." Well, bless her heart. She knew how to make me feel better about a negative situation.

It occurred to me that something called a "Purchase Protection" program with credit cards might allow me to at least reclaim the purchase price of the scarf. When I called VISA's Customer Service, the agent asked, "Do you have a gold VISA card or a regular card?" It so happened that several months earlier, I had been offered a gold card by VISA, but I had declined because I loved the images of the Atlantic puffins on my regular card. "Well, I'm sorry," the agent said, "but the Purchase Protection benefit applies only to gold card holders. Furthermore," she added, "the plan is good only when luggage has been lost after having been checked through on a flight."

To begin my recovery process from this trauma, I sat down and listed everything I could remember having been in the suitcase. In addition to the new scarf and the usual clothes, some of the special items included several other scarves: a unique red-and-navy-blue silk one from Italy that had been a gift from friends; a large square red-and-black paisley wool one, also made in Italy that I had bought at Harrod's in London some years earlier; and a long red-and-black striped Tibetan alpaca scarf and cap from the Tibet Emporium on Mulberry Street in Greenwich Village. I also had in the suitcase several pieces of cherished Celtic and other jewelry—none expensive—along with my camera and three rolls of Paris-exposed film.

In the years since, I have often speculated about what that man did with all my stuff. Did he give it to relatives? If so, did they enjoy wearing the scarves and the jewelry? Did my clothes fit them? Did they know how he obtained them? Or did he try to sell the items? Did he have any idea of the value of the Yves Saint Laurent scarf? Did he ever feel guilty about what he had done? Is he still thieving? Is he in jail? Did he reform?

Not long after this experience, I read an item in *The New York Times* about a woman who believed she had lost her engagement ring in a New York City taxicab. She telephoned the driver about it. He searched his cab but did not find the ring. After his shift was over, however, this caring driver voluntarily retraced his route of that day until he found the ring on a curb at a spot where he had picked up another fare. "I can imagine how she felt," he said at a ceremony honoring his good deed, "so I gave it one more shot." He declined the woman's offer of a reward.

Truly a gem of a fellow! Not all taxi drivers are the same. Would that he had driven me that evening!

*   *   *   *

"HEY, MARY JOY, WOULD YOU be interested in sharing my cabin on a *Queen Elizabeth II* cruise?"

This invitation came from my longtime fine-artist friend, Betty Collins. She regularly taught art classes on the *Queen Elizabeth II* cruises and could invite a friend to share her cabin.

"I sure would."

Ernie, hearing this exchange, chimed in. "If you want to go on a cruise *that* bad, I'll go with you."

Earlier when I had suggested a cruise as a possible vacation option, Ernie's response had always been, "Cruises! I consider them the height of decadence."

Ernie and me on the Veendam Caribbean cruise.

But he yielded this time. So in 1975 we booked passage for a Caribbean/ Bermuda cruise on the *SS Veendam*, one of Holland-American's ships.

As it turns out, Ernie loved it. "The best and most restful vacation I've ever had." He explored the ship from the engine room to the captain's bridge. He watched the flying fish and the dolphins, and he caught up on his reading. The ship's stabilizers forestalled any seasickness. This highly enjoyable sea voyage contrasted sharply with an earlier experience Ernie and I had had.

During Ernie's graduate school days in Gainesville, Florida, during the 1950s, my parents offered to stay with Leslie and

Ernie and me dressed for a formal dinner during our Caribbean cruise.

Denise one weekend, so Ernie and I could get away for a break. We drove to Florida's Gulf Coast—to St. Petersburg and Tarpon Springs. Although neither of us fished as a hobby, Ernie thought it would be fun to go on an all-day deep-sea fishing excursion as observers on a small Greek fishing boat out of Tarpon Springs. We took along a bag lunch.

While the boat chugged along out into the Gulf, we enjoyed watching the small Greek crew at work steering the boat, taking turns slicing off and eating pieces of their round loaf of Greek bread. Then they dropped anchor so folks could fish. That's when the trouble started. The boat began to pitch and rock. A youngster vomited on the deck. The stench caused nausea to overtake most of the passengers. Only the boat's crew ate their lunch. One obese passenger with an extended potbelly propped his fishing pole in a holder in the rigging and lay down on a park bench. His huge potbelly rolled from his crotch to his chest. The sight quenched our appetites. Somehow, neither Ernie nor I upchucked. I wanted to get off, but that was not an option. We were stuck with an all-day excursion. I recalled that day as the longest one of my life.

CEBU cruise boat.

Ernie and I had one of our most enjoyable cruises in August 1982 when we joined four other couples for a week-long holiday aboard a small cruise boat called the *CEBU*. Bobbie and Carl Belson of Bellevue, Washington, operated this "Mom & Pop" cruise for nonsmokers with a crew of only two beside themselves. They flew us in a small seaplane from Seattle north to Cortes Bay, British Columbia, where we boarded their small boat for the cruise south through the scenic Puget Sound and the San Juan Islands in the Strait of Georgia. They stopped at various points to give us day excursions, hikes, and bird watching on shore along the way. We saw many bald eagles as well as cormorants, black oystercatchers, Canada geese, goldfinches, Pine grosbeaks, a yellow-bellied sapsucker woodpecker, swallows, black-capped chickadees, belted kingfishers, gray herons, and an Arctic tern. Seals often frolicked around the boat. We also saw several Indian pictographs in the cliffs.

The crew awakened us in the middle of one night to see an awesome display of the Northern Lights.

The boat moored each night, traveling only during the day. One day Ernie awakened early to pick wild blackberries on Salt Spring Island before we departed. In the late afternoon that day, the tantalizing aroma of freshly baked pie floated around the *CEBU*. Bobbie's assistant cook, Marilyn, made the wild blackberries Ernie had picked into a pie for dessert.

Bobbie Belson prepared varied and delicious meals in her tiny galley. We even had homemade, hand-cranked ice cream once. On the last day of the cruise, Carl, the skipper, invited each guest to take a turn at the wheel as we cruised to Seattle through Puget Sound and the Washington Ship Channel to moorage on Lake Union.

Ernie and I had flown to Seattle a couple days prior to the *CEBU*'s departure to sight-see in that forward-thinking, conservation-minded, "green oriented" city.

After the cruise, we took advantage of being in the Pacific Northwest to hike in the Hoh Rain Forest on the Olympic Peninsula in western Washington State. Some of the Sitka Spruce and Western Hemlock have grown to over 300 feet tall and twenty-three feet in circumference.

Taking my turn at the whell of the CEBU cruise boat.

Spectacular! Hoh is one of the few temperate rain forests in the world and is the largest.

*   *   *   *

TWICE I TRAVELED TO CORNWALL, England, my father's country of origin, to visit relatives descended from my father's siblings. The first time in the fall of 1975, Ernie and I flew to Heathrow Airport near London and before renting a car to drive south to Cornwall, we explored London, using its subway system to get about.

In Cornwall we visited my second cousin, Jenny Dean Jeffrey, and her parents, my cousin Charles Dean and his wife. Charles's father, Jack, was my father's brother. We hit it off with Jenny and her husband, Rodney, who kindly acted as our tour guides, accompanying us to places of interest and sharing pleasant visits to several of Cornwall's fabled pubs.

Cornwall is a gorgeous and historic Celtic place, drawing crowds of tourists during the summers. The province's economy today depends largely on tourist income. A peninsula and the toe of the British boot jutting out from the Southwest corner of England, Cornwall is often referred to as the English Riviera for its beautiful craggy coastline. In many places, though, Cornwall's interior has been badly scarred by mining operations—copper, tin, and open-pit clay mines.

North of Cornwall, in Gloustershire County, we slipped back in history as we viewed the ancient Georgian city of Bath with its Roman remains. But Biburg Village in the Cotswolds, Gloustershire County, with its quaint cottages built of golden limestone, captured me the most.

Some years later, in the fall of 1989, my brother John and I booked passage to England on a trans-Atlantic crossing of the *Queen Elizabeth II*, truly a luxurious floating city. The ship moored at Southhampton seaport, and John and I rented a car to drive to Cornwall.

John had a bone spur on one heel, so I drove first. Unfamiliar with driving on the left side of the road, plus having the steering wheel on the right side of the car, not to mention maneuvering all the British round-abouts, I misjudged the curb and blew a tire. We walked to a phone to call the car rental folks, then waited for them to fetch us and substitute another car. After that, notwithstanding his bone spur, John did all the driving.

Jenny's father, my cousin Charles, had died by then, but once again Jenny and Rodney drove us around. One day they took us to Redruth, Cornwall, to visit another cousin, Nancy Winfred Dean Hitchens (born in 1914). Nancy's father, Thomas George Dean, was another of Dad's brothers. Several people commented that Nancy and I resembled each other.

* * * *

My second cousin Jenny Dean Jeffrey and her husband, Rodney, in Cornwall, England, 1975.

174

The picturesque Cotswolds, Gloustershire, England.

ONE DAY IN 1990, MY ARTIST FRIEND, Betty Collins, a truly seasoned world traveler, called my attention to an advertisement she had seen for a two-week cruise on the Volga River in Russia.

"Let's go," she urged.

"Okay," I agreed.

With my brother, John, on *Queen Elizabeth II*, 1989, headed for England.

President Mikhail Gorbachev had recently declared Perestroika and Glasnost in Russia in an attempt to reform their economic system and restore political, religious, and press freedoms. Part of that initiative was to open up the country again to tourists. Later, in 1998, Tatanya Tolstaya, writing about Gorbachev in *Time* magazine said, "By gently pushing open the gates of reform, he unleashed a democratic flood that deluged the Soviet universe and washed away the Cold War."[15]

So off Betty and I flew from JFK airport in New York to Moscow aboard a Pan Am wide-body 747. I had three seats all to myself, making napping easier on the overnight flight. At the Moscow airport at 10:30 a.m. the next morning, we observed a woman operating the jet-way, maneuvering it to the jetliner's door. A cloudy sky and a nippy temperature of thirty-eight degrees F. greeted us.

A bus took us to Moscow's Riverport, a marina on the Volga River where we boarded the *M/S Russ* cruise ship on a Friday. It carried 332 passengers with a crew of 150. The ship remained moored at the dock until Sunday, while one group left the ship and our group settled in. The cruise ship, immaculately clean and with comfortable cabins, served food that was a far cry from the menu in the Russian Tea Room in New York City. Rather tasteless beef and fish, salami and uncooked bacon with canned peas for breakfast. But they served plenty of fresh fruit that rounded out the meals—apples, pears, and melons.

On Saturday before the cruise on the Volga began, a bus took our group on a tour of Moscow including a stop in Red Square and Cathedral Square in the Kremlin. We learned that the five onion- or helmet-shaped domes on the cathedrals symbolized Matthew, Mark, Luke, and John, plus Jesus. If only three domes, they symbolized the Trinity—Father, Son and Holy Ghost. The shape of the domes helped snow slide off. Gold domes stand for the sun, blue ones for the sky.

We also visited several museums. Trappings of royalty and nobility filled the display cases—embroidered vestments of clergy, the czar's jew-

---

[15]Tatanya Tolstaya, Mikhail Gorbachev, Time magazine, April 13, 1998.

eled crowns, garments, gold and silver chalices, and embroidered gifts from other countries. Russia has more treasures of British craftsmen than England does, because the British melted down all the beautiful gold and silver pieces during the War of the Stuarts.

We stopped by a ballet school. Russian children begin ballet lessons when they are six years old.

On Saturday I walked from the ship to a main highway nearby, crossed over and entered two food stores. The near-empty shelves held only a few cans of food. A bakery had less than a dozen loaves of bread that quickly disappeared. At another store, a long line of people waited for a chance to buy a pathetic-looking piece of beef.

Sunday morning we visited the Russian Orthodox Church of the Holy Trinity, built in the eighteenth century. There are forty-five Russian Orthodox churches in Moscow. Taking pictures of the beautiful interior is forbidden. No one sits. A small group stood in a circle off to the right of the altar, singing beautiful liturgical music.

This cathedral is near Moscow University. Students each plant a tree when they enroll at the university and plant another when they graduate. As a result, the city features lots of trees in its parks and large squares.

At the time I visited, Moscow's population of nine million lived totally in apartments—no private homes at all. The apartment buildings were drab, unattractive, cheap-looking gray buildings, some shabby.

The Russian people expressed warmth and friendship to us at every turn. The cruise took us down the Volga River, stopping at ancient villages and cities along the way from Moscow to Uglitch, to Kostroma, to Ples to Kazmademjanks to Kazan and to Yaraslovl. At each stop a friendly young Russian woman tour-guide greeted us—speaking excellent English—and then showed us points of interest. The intricate architecture of ancient buildings especially fascinated me. Beautiful cathedrals were under restoration after being nearly destroyed under Communist rule.

In Kazan, a beautiful old university town, founded in the thirteenth century, I photographed a statue of Russian poet and hero, Musa Jalil. He participated in the Russian underground resistance to the German fascists in World War II. Because he wore a German uniform as a disguise, some Russians thought he had become a traitor. A fascist spy in the German underground movement revealed to the Germans Jalil's real identity, and the Germans imprisoned him. He continued to write poetry even while in prison; but he was tortured and killed in 1944. A colleague escaped from the prison and told the Russians about Jalil's heroism. The statue honors this Russian poet.

Kazan's population of one million is a mix of European and Asian people—Russian and Muslim Tartars. Kazan, the poet Pushkins's home, boasts ten theaters and twenty museums, as well as many mosques with minarets. Lenin studied at Kazan University, but after he was arrested, he was unable to re-enter the University. So he finished his education by correspondence school with the University of St. Petersburg.

Kazan has trolleys, buses, and taxis and is less drab and has more culture than most of the other cities we visited along the Volga. Our group attended an afternoon concert of Russian (Tartar) folk music at a concert hall at the College of Culture in Kazan. Instead of violins, musicians played balalaikas.

After removing our shoes, we entered a mosque, the only one functioning in Kazan in 1990. In the special hall where women pray separately, some women were softly singing, while another group was having a discussion. Layers of beautiful carpets covered the floor, presents from Muslims in Fin-

Sculpture of Russian poet-hero Musa Jalil in Kazan, Russia.

land. We learned that in 1990 for the first time in fifty years, Muslims in Russia were allowed to send a group to Mecca.

We had just published my daughter Denise's first book, *The Soul of Economies: Spiritual Evolution Goes to the Marketplace*, which she coauthored with her then-husband, Christopher Largent. I had taken several copies with me to Russia. Dr. Anatoli Ivanov, a sociology and lexicology professor at Moscow University, gave several evening lectures on Russia's economy during the cruise. He expressed much interest in Denise's book that I had given him and said he would place it in the University library after reading it. Marina, one of the staff members on the *M/S Russ*, said she would place the copies I gave her in the city libraries in Moscow. Nadya, our Kazan guide, promised to give a copy to the Kazan University library; Natalia in Kostroma did the same.

One evening's special entertainment aboard the ship consisted of a costume party. Betty Collins and I decked ourselves out as Russian nobility—she as Countess Anastasia and me as Princess Eugenie.

Artist friend Betty Collins and me dressed up for a costume party during the Volga River cruise.

A shish-kabob picnic with some of the ship's crew in a pine forest along the Volga River.

Betty related an experience she had had during one of her *Queen Elizabeth II* cruises. She and a friend had been invited to a special captain's reception in one of the ship's lounges prior to dinner. Under a spotlight, Betty managed to sit next to Magnus Pyke, the eccentric British scientist and media figure, who had a booming voice. She had donned a wraparound Indian sari for the occasion. Not realizing that the hem of the sari was caught beneath the leg of her chair, when she stood up to go into dinner, the sari unwound, leaving her standing in only a blouse and her underpants. She swept up the sari from the floor, wrapped it around her, and scurried toward the exit. In his booming voice, Magnus Pyke announced, "Never mind, my love, the invitation said 'dress optional.'"

One day the *M/S Russ* cruise ship anchored at noontime next to a pine forest where we had a picnic featuring shish kabobs. We played games and learned some Russian folk dances.

The weather during our two-week cruise in early October remained mostly cloudy with some light rain almost every day. Temperatures hovered between thirty-five and fifty degrees Fahrenheit.

Larissa, our guide at Yaroslavl, was of Romani descent and was an English major at Yaroslavl University. She expressed great pride in Yaroslavl's Church of Elijah the Prophet. She impressed us with her extensive knowledge of the Bible and history that she demonstrated, as she showed us around Yaroslavl's cathedrals and described the artwork. "People here have not forgotten their religion, though it was forbidden for many years." She told us that during the Communist oppression, her Granny, in the privacy of the family, continued to study and read the Bible aloud and talk about religion. Larissa added, "You can't just think about Communism—there's nothing there."

At the end of our Yaroslavl tour, Larissa asked me to remain behind after everyone else had left the group. We took a walk and talked. Her parents had divorced when she was seven or eight years old. They remain friends, however, she noted. She spent three months in England with a family there and worked as a waitress in a pub. She volunteered to translate *The Soul of Economies* into Russian as a project for her English class. "My

My Russian friend Larisa Alekseevna (left), with sister Tanya and friend, Samantha, Yaroslavl, 1990.

fellow students and I are always eager for something interesting to translate. We need material in English to translate and it is hard to come by." All the English-speaking Russians I encountered said books and magazines in English are highly sought and very scarce. They are hungry for them.

Russian passengers at the rail of moored cruise ships adjacent to ours. The Russian passengers sang to us, reached over to touch hands, and threw kisses—people to people diplomacy.

"Are postal packages opened, inspected, and items taken out?"

"Often they are, but books usually not. Everything is in short supply or not available," she said, "food, clothing, all goods. The department stores are shabby with many empty shelves. Prices are high." When we parted, she handed me a gift, a beautiful wool scarf.

When the ship returned to Moscow it docked at a marina chuck-a-block to another cruise ship—one with all-Russian passengers. They stood at their ship's rail and sang to us as we lined the rail of our ship. They reached across to touch hands with us, even throwing kisses. One of the women gave me a miniature hand-painted Russian doll after I handed her some American dollars. Later, when I unscrewed the doll's head, I found inside a tiny empty perfume vial.

Another tour guide took us on additional sight-seeing in Moscow. We rode the Moscow subway system. The Metro stations of marble and granite featured beautiful mosaic tile floors and pictures on the ceilings, bas-relief designs on the walls, and lovely chandeliers and side-lamp fixtures. A photoelectric beam under the edge of the subway platform automatically halted all trains if anyone fell off the platform onto the tracks.

Beautiful mosaic in Moscow subway station.

At the "Berioska" gift shop in a large Moscow Hotel, I bought a hand-painted lacquered box costing $750! Other mementos I picked up during stops at the various cities included hand-made tatting and lace-trimmed linen items and a hand-embroidered table runner. I also purchased a watercolor painting of an onion-domed cathedral from a young Moscow street artist.

Today, in 2007 as I write this, I learned that since Vladimer Putin became president in 2000, most of the freedoms instituted by Gorbachev have been radically curtailed. In fact, former world chess champion and opposition activist, Garry Kasparov, has stated that Russia today is no longer a democracy but a police state once again.

* * * *

IN CHAPTER 14, I MENTIONED the trips I took to Prague in the Czech Republic and to Killarney, Ireland, in 1992 and 1994 to attend conferences of the International Transpersonal Association. Steeped in history, the ancient city of Prague takes visitors back centuries with its architecture. It is purported to be the best-preserved city in Europe. One of the speakers at the Conference, a spiritual leader, along with his wife (both barefoot), took a small group of us on a tour of sacred places in Prague during an off-time from the Conference. One place we visited offered me an especially memorable experience. In a 1,000-year-old chapel, the strong essence of antiquity enveloped me as I sat in a pew meditating. I could feel the presence of spiritual seekers down through the centuries—souls who had worshipped in that place.

Musicians and artists lined both sides of the Charles Bridge in Prague. As a memento, I bought a watercolor painting of one of Prague's ancient cathedrals from a street artist on the Bridge. Framed, it adorns a bookshelf in my bedroom.

The 1994 Conference found me in green, green Killarney, in southern Ireland, the Emerald Isle. Misty and moisty, the country bursts with colorful parks, flower gardens, and window boxes everywhere. Unfortunately, I was unable to visit Donegal in Northern Ireland, which had been the hometown of my maternal grandfather's parents before they immigrated to the United States.

* * * *

DURING THE SIXTEEN YEARS I WORKED for the National Audubon Society, whenever quarterly Board meetings convened in locations other than New York City, several other senior staff members and I traveled to the far-flung meeting sites. These Board meetings, usually during a long weekend, comprised committee meetings and a full Board meeting. In addition, a birding field trip to a nearby wildlife refuge or Audubon sanctuary filled most of one day. Tightly scheduled as they were with Audubon business, these weekends allowed scant opportunity to explore the places we went. So while I can say that I have been to Winnipeg, San Francisco, Los Angeles, Hawaii, Greenwich, Connecticut, Ft. Myers, Florida, New Orleans, San Antonio, Maine, North Dakota, and a number of other places, I could not spend much time sight-seeing or learning about these places. I don't feel as if I have really "been there." The 1990 trip to Costa Rica, however, stands out as an exception. The National Audubon Society pre-

Peter Berle presenting an Audubon Medal to Costa Rica President Dr. Oscar Arias Sanchez (second from left), Costa Rica, 1990.

sented Dr. Oscar Arias Sanchez, president from 1986 to 1990, the Audubon Medal for his policies and actions relating to protecting the environment. Dr. Sanchez later received the Nobel Peace Prize. In 2006, Dr. Sanchez was once again elected Costa Rica's president.

Our field trip while in Costa Rica consisted of a birding hike in the lush tropical Monteverdi Rain Forest led by then-Audubon biologist George Powell. He identified and pointed out to us forty-six different bird species. Excitement ran highest when we spotted a Quetzal or resplendent trogon, considered a rare jewel in the bird world. Truly a peak experience!

*   *   *   *

AFTER RETIRING FROM AUDUBON in August of 1995, and before plunging into researching and writing *Women Pioneers for the Environment*, I redeemed my winning Audubon raffle prize and flew up to New Brunswick for a holiday. The all-paid-for trip included not only air fare but also a rental car, bed-and-breakfast accommodations, and a whale-watching excursion from Seal Cove Harbor—the highlight of this holiday. My friend and I saw more of the endangered Atlantic right whales than we could count. These awesome creatures swam close to our boat—close enough so we caught wisps

A picturesque covered bridge, New Brunswick.

of their fishy-smelling breath when they "blew," evoking "Ohs" and "Ahs" among our group, especially when the whales then dived and flipped their tails out of the water. Many species of whales, dolphins, and porpoises swim the waters along the New Brunswick coastline. The tour guide told us that Humpbacks often weigh as much as a house.

During this pelagic excursion, we also saw a number of birds, including herring gulls, shearwaters, terns, Atlantic puffins, and cormorants. We also spotted a majestic bald eagle perched on the top-most pinnacle of a rocky island we passed.

We spent two days in a rustic cottage on Grand Manan Island. Well-known author Willa Cather spent many of her summers there writing her novels. This cottage made birding effortless. Just standing on the back porch one morning, I saw a flock of cedar waxwings, several pairs of American goldfinches, and a black-and-white warbler.

Lobster fishing is big business in New Brunswick's Atlantic coastal villages, and stacks of lobster traps were everywhere.

I have an affinity for lighthouses, and so I sought out and photographed some of them along the province's Atlantic coast.

*   *   *   *

Stacks of shrimp traps, New Brunswick.

One of New Brunswick's many lighthouses.

SINCE RELOCATING TO ST. PAUL, Minnesota, in 2000, I have done little traveling. But in 2001, Jeannine and I flew to Maine for a pleasant long weekend. We moseyed our way along the coast in a rental car, browsing in old villages' general stores and antique shops with their creaking wooden floors.

In 2003, Jeannine and I spent another relaxing long weekend together in Duluth on Minnesota's North Shore with its famous lift bridge. She helped me pick out some clip earrings made from agates from Lake Superior. I wear them almost every day.

Jeannine during a weekend holiday in Maine with me, early 2001.

Chapter 18

Celtic Consequences and Other Calamities

ORGET THE PHYSICAL THERAPY," Dr. Mumtaz Kazim, my general practitioner exclaimed in alarm. "I'm afraid you have temporal arteritis (TA) and polymyalgia rheumatica (PMR), which often accompanies it."

"What in the world is that?"

"It's inflammation of the arteries—a very serious condition."

Scratching out a prescription for the so-called wonder drug prednisone, she added, "Have this filled immediately and take sixty milligrams with some milk as soon as you get home. In the meantime, I'll make arrangements for you to have a biopsy first thing tomorrow morning to confirm my diagnosis."

During the fall of 2001, my back, shoulder and leg muscles and joints became so stiff and achy I couldn't get out of bed in the morning without help from Denise.

At the same time, eating and chewing became painful, and I lost ten pounds. Furthermore, I began having severe sharp, jabbing pains in my temples. The pain was so intense that I couldn't function without Advil. During my entire life, I had never been subject to headaches.

Because I had been working in the garden, I speculated that I must have strained some muscles and tendons. Thinking physical therapy might help, I picked a therapist out of the yellow pages.

"I can't help you without a prescription from your doctor," the physical therapist told me.

So when I requested a P.T. prescription on December 13, 2001, from Dr. Kazim, I casually mentioned the severe temple headaches, triggering her instant diagnosis of TA and PMR. Only later did I learn the reason for her alarm.

I took the prednisone around four o'clock that afternoon. At midnight I awakened drenched with sweat, including my hair. I leaped out of bed—totally free from the muscular and joint pain and the headache—took a shower and went back to bed.

Early the next morning, Denise and I arrived at the Minnesota Vascular Institute for the biopsy. The surgeon was late. With me in a hospital gown and paper booties, Denise and I waited in a small room with a sign on the door, "Mary Breton."

"They have my name wrong," I complained.

"It doesn't matter," Denise replied, but the worried look on her face made me sense that she was withholding information from me.

The surgeon arrived and I entered the operating room. I had never been in an operating room before—a scary experience. The bright lights, a bevy of nurses bustling about, preparing me for the biopsy by shaving the hair back from my temples, covering me with warm flannel blankets.

Then the surgeon approached. "Which temple is the worst pain-wise?"

"My left."

"Okay, we'll do the biopsy there first. It may not be necessary to do the other side."

After administering a local anesthetic, he made an incision in my left temple, taking a section of artery to analyze.

"You stay right there on the operating table," he said, "while I go over to the lab nearby and analyze this artery. I'll be back."

The nurses hovered around, eager to keep me warm and comfortable, endeavoring to allay my anxiety. Thinking back, their kindness and warmth, along with the surgeon's gentleness and caring attitude, gave me a positive perspective on the medical world I hadn't had before, enabling me to take in my stride several subsequent surgical procedures in 2003 and 2004. After about twenty minutes, the surgeon reappeared.

"Dr. Kazim diagnosed your condition correctly," he said, "and I have called and told her so. I also told your daughter, Denise."

Later Denise revealed to me what I had not known. She had asked the surgeon if I was out of danger. He assured her I would be okay. The hazards involved with temporal arteritis are that, unless it is diagnosed and treated promptly, it can result in a stroke or blindness. When we next saw Dr. Kazim, she related a sad story. During one weekend, a woman called in to a clinic where Dr. Kazim had been working at the time, complaining of a severe headache. The doctor on weekend duty (not Dr. Kazim) told the woman by phone to take some Tylenol. By Monday, she was blind. The condition was irreversible.

While prednisone allayed the headaches and muscle pain, this drug can have numerous side effects. Dr. Kazim prescribed medications to forestall most of them.

I made the mistake of having a permanent wave soon after beginning to take prednisone. My hair began to fall out.

Dr. Kazim recommended that we see a temporal arteritis specialist. After some extensive Internet research, Jeannine identified a German physician—Dr. Cornelia Weyand, a rheumatologist at the Mayo Clinic in Rochester, Minnesota. Even though Dr. Weyand was devoting most of her time to research, authoring articles for medical journals and lecturing at conferences and had not been accepting new patients, she agreed to see me.

Dr, Weyand, a tall, dark-haired, friendly woman, always wore a business suit, never a white coat like most physicians. "What is your heritage?" her first question.

"My father came from Cornwall, England, and my maternal grandfather's parents came from Northern Ireland." As she questioned me further, I told her about the difficulty I had chewing and eating. "That's called jaw claudication," she replied, "and it's another manifestation of TA."

"You're a textbook case, I must say. TA strikes women over fifty of Northern European heritage, who have a strong immune system, and have always enjoyed good health," she told me.

"What? That doesn't sound exactly fair."

"No, it doesn't," she agreed, "but just make friends with the condition and we'll deal with it."

So my Celtic heritage also had its negative consequences. In between visits to Dr. Weyand at the Mayo Clinic, Dr. Kazim monitored my progress with regular blood tests and examinations. I learned that rest, exercise, and avoidance of stress helped recovery. I stopped watching the depressing war news on TV. I also learned that the body's adrenal glands produce natural cortisone, but they reduce the level or stop producing it when a person is on the artificial cortisone, prednisone. This means that one cannot reduce the daily dosage of prednisone too rapidly but must come down in small increments to give the adrenal glands time to gradually kick in again.

Along the way in 2002 and early 2003, my visits to Dr. Weyand involved, among other procedures, an ultrasound and blood tests. She asked for and I consented to her taking extra blood samples for her research work. In late 2003, Dr. Weyand resigned from the Mayo Clinic to accept a prestigious position at Emory University in Atlanta.

In the meantime, Denise researched supplements that would be beneficial and established a regimen for me that helped advance my recovery and enhance my health.

*   *   *   *

AFTER USING CHRISTIAN SCIENCE for healing most of my life, the medical world had always been completely foreign to me. However, my experiences beginning in 2001 totally changed my attitude toward doctors and hospitals. I have gained enormous respect and appreciation for their skill and for their caring attitude. Two years later, I had another experience of being saved by modern medicine.

Wracked with pain and clad only in my bra and panties—with the left leg of my gardening jeans crumpled at my left ankle, still tucked into the top of my sock—I lay on the basement floor. I couldn't move or get up. But I dragged myself a couple feet to the basement stairs where I rested my head on the bottom step.

In the early morning of July 21, 2003. I had gone outside to do some gardening in the yard of our bungalow in St. Paul. To prevent mosquitoes from biting my ankles, I had tucked the hems of my jeans inside my socks.

Descending to the basement to shed my gardening duds, I tried to shake off my jeans while standing on only one leg and without holding onto anything. It worked okay with my right leg, but when I tried shaking the jeans off my left leg, I lost my balance and fell flat backwards onto the concrete floor.

The pain was so severe I knew I had broken something. A small green watering can lay on the floor within reach. I grabbed it and begin banging on the stair wall, hoping Denise in her room two floors above me would hear the banging and investigate. But an hour passed before she came down and discovered me, nearly naked at the foot of the basement stairs.

"I can't move. I think I've broken something. Can you finish taking the jeans off my left ankle?"

"Okay, but first let me call 911. I heard the banging, but thought you were just puttering around in the basement." While waiting for the ambulance, she covered me with a nightie and eased the jeans off my left ankle. Seconds later a crew of male medics arrived with an ambulance in our alley to take me to the United Hospital emergency room in St. Paul. An x-ray revealed a broken left hip. A nurse installed a catheter and gave me a sedative to ease the fierce pain a bit.

Fortunately, a slot opened that same afternoon in Dr. Jonathan Bieble's schedule, which allowed him to perform hip replacement surgery on me right away.

The morphine they gave me resulted in hallucinations. After the operation, when I became semi-conscious, I saw that my knees had been strapped around a wedge-shaped Styrofoam "pillow." I learned later that it is called an "abductor." The purpose was to keep the new artificial metal hip in place. Hallucinations from the morphine lasted all night. I feared aliens were binding me up to abduct me.

Hospital stays offer scant time to sleep or rest, especially if a patient is not in a private room. Around the clock, every four hours, a nurse comes by to take all one's vital signs. The lights dim a bit, but never go off at night. The bustling of staff continues round the clock.

Once the catheter was disconnected, I had to ring for a nurse to come unstrap my legs and help me to the bathroom, after which the nurse strapped up my legs again. I remained in the hospital for four days. In the middle of one night when I rang for a nurse, I looked up to see a black male face bending over me, asking me what I needed. He wore a tiger-tooth necklace. No one had told me that a black male nurse would be on night duty. Already fragile mentally and emotionally from the surgery and hallucinations, his appearance scared me. Later I learned he was from Liberia, a fine young man, very caring and helpful. What a moment to confront my racial programming as a white woman to fear men of color!

A rehabilitation specialist made a number of house calls once I returned home, teaching me exercises to hasten recovery. I used a walker for a couple weeks, then a cane, and before long I didn't need either. I saw Dr. Bieble for a couple follow-up appointments in the ensuing weeks, and then again one year after the surgery.

A friend of Denise's had hip surgery in 2008, and we learned from her that much has changed since 2003 in the medical technology relating to hip replacements. The size of the incision had been much reduced and no muscle now needs to be cut. And this friend didn't need to have her knees strapped to an abductor pillow. All good news!

*   *   *   *

AFTER DR. WEYAND LEFT the Mayo Clinic, Dr. Kazim recommended that I see another rheumatology specialist in the Twin Cities to monitor my reduction schedule of prednisone. She referred me to Dr. Paul Waytz of Edina, whom I began seeing regularly in January 2004.

In the meantime, because of cataracts in my eyes, I became nervous about driving. Reading road signs was difficult. So, early in March of

2004, Dr. Scott McKee of the St. Paul Eye Clinic removed cataracts from my right eye and at the end of April from my left eye.

Prior to the cataract surgery, arthritis in my right knee became progressively worse in spite of acupuncture and chiropractic treatments. I began having to use a cane. Finally, in September 2004, I consulted Dr. Owen O'Neill, an orthopedic specialist who, after examining an x-ray of my knee, recommended knee replacement surgery.

However, other problems made it necessary to postpone knee surgery. I experienced another bout with diverticulitis on a weekend. A doctor on weekend duty at a nearby Urgent Care facility prescribed an antibiotic that gave me extreme nausea and diarrhea.

In the middle of the night, my bladder failed. With my bed and nightclothes soaked, I headed for the bathroom to change. When I tried to walk back to my bed, I fainted, falling to the floor. Denise heard the thump and dashed downstairs. She called 911.

"She's badly dehydrated," the ER crew told Denise. "And that antibiotic is too strong for her." They hooked me up to tubes to replace my body fluids and gave me a milder antibiotic intravenously.

A neurologist, ordered a CAT scan and MRI. These revealed that I had a condition called normal pressure hydrocephalus—excess fluid on the brain. Symptoms include incontinence, a shuffling walk, and memory problems. Prednisone changes the fluid action in the body, Dr. Weyand had told us, and so we wondered if this was another side effect.

We were referred to Dr. Mahmoud Nagib, a neurology specialist and surgeon.

"Walk along the hall ahead of me to my office," Dr. Nagib directed. "I've been watching people walk for over twenty years and can easily spot those with normal pressure hydrocephalus. Doctors often misdiagnose it." Dr. Nagib recommended brain surgery to install a programmable shunt in my brain that would drain away the excess fluid and carry it to my stomach through an internal tube. He explained to Denise and me in detail the procedure and how it would work.

So, on Monday, October 25, 2004, I had the brain surgery. It involved two incisions—one in the back of my head and the other in my abdomen where the internal drain tube was connected to my stomach. I remained in the Abbott Northwestern Hospital three days. A week later, Dr. Nagib's nurse practitioner, Sharon Erickson, removed the sutures from both incisions. But during the next several weeks I suffered severe headaches and nausea. It turned out that at the time of the surgery, the shunt had been programmed to drain away too much fluid. Following adjustment of the programmable shunt a couple times, my recovery speeded up.

Eager to have all these surgeries over with, I then scheduled the right knee replacement surgery with Dr. Owen O'Neill for December 1, 2004, less than six weeks after the brain surgery. In the rehabilitation center the day after the knee surgery, the therapist took me into the kitchen. "You're going to make brownies." She must be kidding I thought, I'm ambulating with a walker. But she wasn't kidding.

"Here's a brownie mix package. You'll do fine," and she left me to cope alone.

After my discharge from the Rehab Center, once again nurse-therapists made house calls twice a week for almost a month, teaching me a series of exercises and taking measurements of my increasing knee flexibility.

Denise and Jeannine teased me: "If this pattern continues you're going to be our bionic woman."

*   *   *   *

SO NOW, IN 2013, notwithstanding a bit of arthritis in my hands, I feel really good. I am able to garden, cook, houseclean, do laundry, and drive the car to shop for groceries. As well, I serve as secretary-treasurer, marketing researcher, and proof-reader for our nonprofit publishing business. The opportunity to work as a volunteer for Living Justice Press has given me a deep and satisfying sense of purpose. I like to think of the work we do as a kind of trim tab, influencing our culture one individual and one organization at a time, moving us toward greater social justice all around. This purpose keeps me energized and happy. I hope to continue working for several more decades. We shall see.

Here's a quote from Edward Everett Hale I keep displayed on my computer: "I am only one, but I am one. I cannot do everything, but I can do something. And I will not let what I cannot do interfere with what I can do."

℘The End℘